SCHOOL LIBRARY MEDIA SERIES
Edited by Diane de Cordova Biesel

1. *Chalk Talk Stories*, written and illustrated by Arden Druce, 1993.
2. *Toddler Storytime Programs*, by Diane Briggs, 1993.
3. *Alphabet: A Handbook of ABC Books and Book Extensions for the Elementary Classroom*, 2nd ed., by Patricia L. Roberts, 1994.
4. *Cultural Cobblestones: Teaching Cultural Diversity*, by Lynda Miller, Theresa Steinlage, and Mike Printz, 1994.
5. *ABC Books and Activities: From Preschool to High School*, by Cathie Hilterbran Cooper, 1996.
6. *Zoolutions: A Mathematical Expedition with Topics for Grades 4 through 8*, by Anne Burgunder and Vaunda Nelson, 1996.
7. *Library Lessons for Grades 7–9*, by Arden Druce, 1997.
8. *Counting Your Way through 1–2–3 Books and Activities*, by Cathie Hilterbran Cooper, 1997.
9. *Art and Children: Using Literature to Expand Creativity*, by Robin W. Davis, 1996.
10. *Story Programs: A Source Book of Materials*, 2nd ed., by Carolyn Sue Peterson and Ann Fenton, 1999.
11. *Taking Humor Seriously in Children's Literature: Literature-Based Mini-Units and Humorous Books for Children Ages 5–12*, by Patricia L. Roberts, 1997.
12. *Multicultural Friendship Stories and Activities for Children, Ages 5–14*, by Patricia L. Roberts, 1997.
13. *Side by Side: Twelve Multicultural Puppet Plays*, by Jean M. Pollock, 1997.
14. *Reading Fun: Quick and Easy Activities for the School Library Media Center*, by Mona Kerby, 1997.
15. *Paper Bag Puppets*, by Arden Druce with illustrations by Geraldine Hulbert, Cynthia Johnson, Harvey H. Lively, and Carol Ditter Waters, 1999.
16. *Once Upon a Childhood: Fingerplays, Action Rhymes, and Fun Times for the Very Young*, by Dolores C. Chupela, 1998.
17. *Bulletin Bored? or Bulletin Boards!: K–12*, by Patricia Sivak and Mary Anne Passatore, 1998.
18. *Color and Shape Books for All Ages*, by Cathie Hilterbran Cooper, 1998.
19. *Big Books for Little Readers*, by Robin W. Davis, 1999.

Big Books
for Little Readers

Robin W. Davis

School Library Media Series, No. 19

The Scarecrow Press, Inc.
Lanham, Maryland, and London
1999

SCARECROW PRESS, INC.

Published in the United States of America
by Scarecrow Press, Inc.
4720 Boston Way
Lanham, Maryland 20706

4 Pleydell Gardens, Folkestone
Kent CT20 2DN, England

British Library Cataloguing in Publication Information Available

Library of Congress Cataloging-in-Publication Data

Davis, Robin Works, 1962–
    Big Books for little readers / Robin W. Davis.
      p. cm. — (School library media series ; no. 19)
    Includes bibliographical references and index.
    ISBN 0-8108-3621-1 (alk. paper)
    1. Libraries—United States—Special collections—Big books
(Children's books). I. Title. II. Series.
Z688.B52D38   1999
025.3'49—dc21   98-50933
                                      CIP

∞™ The paper used in this publication meets the minimum requirements of
American National Standard for Information Sciences—Permanence of
Paper for Printed Library Materials, ANSI/NISO Z39.48–1992.
Manufactured in the United States of America.

Contents

Editor's Foreword by *Diane de Cordova Biesel*   vii

1   Introduction: Who Put the BIG in Big Books?   1

2   Shared Reading Experiences and Big Books   3

3   How Big Is Big? Problems of Big Books   5

4   Practical Advice: Storing, Circulating, Preserving, and Displaying Big Books   7

5   Using Big Books in Story Times and Programs   13

6   Conclusion and Selected Bibliography   73

7   Annotated Bibliography of Recommended Big Books with Age Levels   75

Appendix: Big Book Publishing Sources   95

Index   99

About the Author   101

Editor's Foreword

The School Library Media Series is directed to the school library media specialist, particularly the building-level librarian. The multifaceted role of the librarian as educator, collection developer, curriculum developer, and information specialist is examined. The series includes concise, practical books on topical and current subjects related to programs and services.

What are Big Books? Where did they come from? How should they be used with the prereading crowd?

In *Big Books for Little Readers* Robin W. Davis explores this significant trend in the teaching of reading. The sections that include practical suggestions for the maintenance and storage of Big Books will also be of particular interest.

Diane de Cordova Biesel
Series Editor

Chapter 1

Introduction: Who Put the BIG in Big Books?

Have you ever wondered about Big Books? Which Big Books are well designed, and which are merely oversized? How do you use Big Books in story programs or in the classroom? If you have wondered, this book is for you. This reference will explore:

- The shared reading experience.

- Failures and successes of enlarging text and illustrations.

- Practicalities of purchasing and using Big Books.

- Ideas for activities using Big Books.

- Patterns for suggested activities.

- Sources for Big Books and bibliography.

Enlarged texts, or Big Books, allow groups of children to see and respond to the printed page and pictures of a story as they would during a one-on-one lap reading with an adult. Big Books began in the late 1960s in New Zealand, where teacher-created enlarged texts were used to inspire children lacking in reading skills or confidence. These books encouraged a shared reading experience in which the story was read as a group. In 1979, Don Holdaway, the well-known and respected researcher, began designing and conducting activities with children that involved enlarged texts.[1] These activities inspired publishers to produce Big Books.

Big Books are said to build on the natural experiences that most children have with print, especially lap reading with an adult. They also take into consideration the print children are exposed to in the environment, such as signs, advertisements, and television. These versions of print, says Holdaway, are "large, colorful, and well designed."[2]

A Selection Criteria

The Big Books included in the bibliography at the end of this volume were selected based on their appeal to the listed age group, usefulness for group sharing, quality of construction, and success of translation from small to large format if a small version exists. If the book is not a primary purchase, the annotation indicates this. For reviews of Big Books, see the following sources.

Carter, Betty. "Fall Roundup." *Book Links* (November 1994): 58–60.
———. "Big Books." *Book Links* (November 1995): 59–62.

1. For more information on the work of Don Holdaway, who is considered the father of many innovative methods of teaching reading, see his book *Foundations of Literacy* (Heinemann, 1979).

2. Barbara Park, "The Big Book Trend—A Discussion with Don Holdaway," *Language Arts* 59, no. 8 (November/December 1982).

Carter, Betty, and James L. Thomas. "Big Books: Purchasing and Using Enlarged Texts." *Book Links* (November 1991): 15–17.

Donahue, Richard. "Books Big and Small." *Publishers Weekly* (February 12, 1992): 13–15.

Friedland, Jeni. "The Big Book Buying Guide." *Instructor* (October 1991): 22.

Irwin, Christine. "Small Children Fall for Big Books." *Instructor* (October 1991): 21.

Moss, Barbara. "Big Books." *Bookbag Magazine* (August 1996): 54–55.

Chapter 2

Shared Reading Experiences and Big Books

A child's picture book is essentially a work of visual art—something that speaks directly to the eye. Its role is to stimulate the imagination through the eye—to educate a child in the true sense—by drawing something out of the observer. Effective sharing of literature depends on books that involve the child in this way. One way to do this is the shared reading experience, which is simply that time-tested reading approach that parents, teachers, and librarians have used for generations at story time or at bedtime. Shared reading experiences help us get back to basics by highlighting reading as the communication activity that it is. Shared reading is nothing really complicated or new. In it you share enjoyment; awareness of how print works; repetitious, rhyming, humorous, and dramatic language; predictions; and associated activities with the children.

Big Books can help establish a special, specific time during which children develop the interest, enthusiasm, and concepts that help them become successful readers. When a teacher or librarian reads a book that is large in size and has large print, the children enjoy the same kind of reading experience in a group that they might have one-on-one at home, sitting in a parent's lap and focusing on the text and illustrations. They can talk about the pictures and print, ask questions, and make predictions about the story. Thus the reading process becomes a more personalized experience for children. Research shows us that one common experience of all good readers is that they were read to in this way as young children.[3] These children see story sharing as a time for fun, a time to be nurtured, a time of security, and a time to explore new things. Big Books are a way for teachers and librarians to try to replicate this personal method of story sharing and to involve children in the print and pictures of a book. We can't totally replicate the lap story method of shared reading, but we can surround the child with print, provide a welcoming reading environment, encourage interaction with the story, and promote independent time with books. Big Books can be used in these ways during a regular story time or sharing session.

Shared reading using Big Books has four components: discovery, exploration, extension, and independent experience.

Discovery

Discovery sets the stage for the initial sharing of the story. Displaying the Big Book on an easel for a few minutes before you share the story can generate excitement. When you are

---

3. See E. Suzby, "The Development of the Young Child and the Emergence of Literacy," in *Handbook of Research on Teaching the Language Arts*, ed. J. Flood, M. Jensen, D. Lapp, and J. R. Squire (Macmillan, 1991); and W. H. Teale and E. Suzby, eds., *Emergent Literacy: Writing and Reading* (Ablex, 1986).

ready, settle the children comfortably around you. (Be sure to read the book yourself before you share it with the children.) Read the title and introduce the author. Point out the illustrations on the cover, and ask the children to make predictions about the book based on the cover picture and title. Read the whole story through. It is important that your reading reflect your enjoyment and delight in the story: read with enthusiasm; convey the full impact of the story dramatically with your voice and gestures; if there are repetitive words or phrases, invite the children to join in. Pick one or two comfortable spots in the story and stop there to let the children predict what will happen on the next page. Point to the pictures and words when it seems natural. After reading, invite reactions and discussion to this first encounter. Did the children like the story? Allow the children to confirm or change their predictions about the book.

Exploration

Exploration involves discovering any additional treasures or elements about a Big Book. Look back at favorite illustrations and recap the tale. Encourage the children to look carefully for details and to savor the pictures. Reread sentences that are appealing or repetitive, and pause before predictable words to let children fill them in. Next, ask the children a question that will help them derive meaning from the text. Use the story as a jumping-off point for the children to share rich memories and experiences from their own lives. An excellent way to make reading and writing more meaningful is to write a question at the top of a posterboard or large sheet of paper and to record the children's answers. They get to see their words in print, and it is fun to display for

parents to read. Some examples are: Where does this story take place? What do you know about _____? (Fill in the blank with an appropriate animal, person, or object from the story you wish to explore.) How else could this story end? What other books have you read about _____?

Extension

Good books are springboards for rich experiences with a wide range of appeal. Extensions should be seen not as extras but as an essential part of story sharing. Extensions include writing experiences, creative drama, art or craft, movement, curriculum activities (math, science, social studies, history), music, cooking, language experience, culture experience, and author studies.

Independent Experience

Independence is the drive that children have for mastery of reading skills and the enjoyment they derive from exploring favorite books over and over. Make sure additional copies of the book in small or Big Book format are on hand for children to check out and take home. An excellent way to get children reading is to tell them to share the story with their parents or siblings. Another idea is to make available a commercially or teacher-produced audiotape of the story for children to follow along with in the book or share with others. Blank tapes could also be provided for families to make their own recordings of the book. Give the children a list of books related to this shared reading and encourage parents to read new books with them.

Chapter 3

How Big Is Big? Problems of Big Books

Storage and Price

The most obvious problems with Big Books are their storage and price. The majority of Big Books are about 15 inches × 18 inches or larger, leading to questions about how and where to store them. Chapter 4, "Practical Advice: Storing, Circulating, Preserving, and Displaying Big Books" addresses these storage problems. With prices ranging from $16.95 to $30.00, the cost of buying these books is a major factor when considering a purchase. Big Books should be considered for purchase despite the cost problem if:

- You have large groups of children (more than twenty) in groups for story time or shared reading at one time.

- You are seeking a way to add variety or interest to your book-sharing programs.

- There is a large group of teachers in your school or community who would borrow, suggest, and support the addition of Big Books to the library.

Translation from Original Format to Big Book

The Big Book should follow the same layout, color, illustration, and wording as the original. Some stories work well as a small text but lose certain qualities when enlarged. A good example of this is *The Tale of Peter Rabbit* by Beatrix Potter (Scholastic, 1986). The story's original, small size contributes to the intimate quality of this tale, which is lost when the book is enlarged. Stories with very intricate illustrations can also lose detail when they are made into Big Books. An example of such a book is *All the Pretty Horses* by Susan Jeffers (Scholastic, 1987). The delicate line drawings lose their detail and become fuzzy when enlarged.

Quality of Original Big Books

Judge these books by the same standards you use for regular size picture books; don't add one to your collection simply because it is big.

Construction

Since Big Books usually come in paperback form, many are poorly bound or are simply saddle-stitched (cover and pages are stapled together on spine). Some companies sell prebound books, but their cost is very high.

Chapter 4

Practical Advice: Storing, Circulating, Preserving, and Displaying Big Books

Ideas for Storing and Displaying Big Books

Finding a practical method to store and display Big Books, whether for your own use or for circulation, is one of the major obstacles to their use. The large, paper format of most Big Books makes them hard to store, easy to damage, and a challenge to display. But an attractive display of Big Books helps build excitement and encourage reading. The following are options and suggestions for both storage and display. Prices are given for comparative purposes only; actual costs may vary.

Products Specifically Designed to Hold Big Books

- Bredford offers an atlas or Big Book storage cabinet for $319.95 that stores and organizes about two hundred Big Books in horizontal format. It features eight slide-out steel shelves that measure 23 inches by 26½ inches. It is set on casters and will hold a table-top easel for display of one Big Book. Available from Demco, 1-800-356-1200.

- Big Book Truck—This new, red metal truck features a hinged, pull-out display. The 27 inch × 16 inch shelf tilts down for viewing one Big Book. The truck has five oversized dividers on the bottom shelf to hold Big Books upright. It will hold sixty to one hundred Big Books for storage. Cost is $300.00 from Highsmith Company, 1-800-558-2110.

- Big Book House—This shelf is made of masonite and wire, with five 27 inch × 19 inch shelves. The roof of the house doubles as a display easel, but is too low for book sharing. It will display about four to six books and store thirty to fifty. Available for $200.00 from Demco, 1-800-356-1200.

- A Big Book Tree is available from Scholastic (1-800-724-6527) for $135.00. The tree stands 5'9" tall and includes an Allen wrench for easy assembly. This rack is decorated to look like an apple tree. Its two "branches" will hold about twenty Big Books in bags. Scholastic carries sets of ten plastic Big Book bags for $19.00.

- A Big Book Tree is also available from Teaching Resource Center (P.O. Box 1509, San Leandro, CA 94577, 1-800-833-3389). This wooden rack is made to hold up to twelve bags of Big Books. Sturdy, plastic Tree Bags are available at an additional charge; each bag holds several books. The tree is 4 feet tall and 36 inches wide. Cost is $80.00 for the tree, $119.95 for six bags. This item is less expensive than other items for storage, but the cost of the bags may make it unfeasible for some. These bags are much more expensive than those from Scholastic. They are a heavier grade of plastic and have sturdier handles.

- Highsmith (1-800-558-2110) makes a very nice Big Book storage system that was designed by a librarian. This cart has hardboard dividers and wheels and will hold one hundred or more books. A full-width label channel runs across the top so your collection can be organized and identified. The unit is made of particle board and measures 33 inches high by 36 inches wide by 18 inches deep. Cost is $590.00. For an additional charge of $106.00, a master-index, flip-style card file is available. You can display one to three Big Books on top of the unit by using tabletop easels.

- ABC School Supply (1-800-669-4222) offers a Big Book storage and display unit for $105.00. This unit is 30 inches deep, 12 inches wide, 22 inches high and contains four divided compartments. It is mounted on casters and holds one hundred books.

Other Ways to Store Big Books

The least expensive way to store Big Books is to devise your own container by reusing the boxes the books are shipped in. After saving a quantity of boxes, cut off one end of each. Use heavy, clear tape to reinforce each box. Then, with the opened end of each box facing up, hot glue the boxes together. Place two or three Big Books in each section. The only cost is for tape and hot glue.

Artwork stacking trays are interlocking, plastic, oversized trays that measure 24 inches × 36 inches. Each tray holds five to eight Big Books for storage. They are available from art-supply catalogs and stores and cost about $90.00 each. Or you can look into an artwork storage cabinet, which is a five-tray metal cabinet with trays 24 inches × 26 inches. It will hold about thirty Big Books for storage. There is room to display one or two Big Books on top of the cabinet if you purchase easels. Cost is about $200.00 from art supply catalogs and stores.

An interesting way to store and/or display Big Books in a closet or on a metal rack is to use plastic skirt hangers. Available from retail stores, you simply use the hangers to hang the Big Books as you would items of clothing from the attached clips. Try to get the metal hangers with rubber-coated clips; these are the strongest, and the rubber coating will help prevent dents in the books from the clips. Plastic hangers of this type will not work if the clips are plastic.

One school library uses stuffed animal "nets" to store and display their Big Books. These mesh nets hang in a corner from nails or hooks. They can be purchased at a toy store for about $12.00 each.

Another item available from Teaching Resources Center is a deluxe, wheeled easel that has a pocket chart, felt board, dry erase board, a Big Book attachment with a Big Book storage box that attaches conveniently to the bottom of the 5-foot-tall easel. The box is 31 inches wide and will hold twenty to forty Big Books, or twenty Big Books and ten to fifteen regular-sized books. It is very convenient for story-time sharing, especially if equipment must be moved from place to place. It costs $180.00.

Magazine face-out shelving/display costs $100.00 and up for a small wire rack that holds fifteen to thirty Big Books. Wooden shelves of this kind that display about twelve

Big Books run $300.00 and up. These are available from library-supply companies in various styles and sizes. Some have storage space underneath the display shelving.

A newspaper stand with rods is another unique but expensive way to hang Big Books. Single- or double-faced racks that hold ten or more wooden newspaper rods cost $300.00 and up. The books hang sideways with the newspaper rod through the center. This is not the best method when damage to binding is considered, but if you have a rack of this type, it may be used.

You can purchase a poster display stand from Gaylord (1-800-448-6160) for $110.00. This metal stand both stores and displays Big Books. It is lightweight, space efficient and has wheels. It measures 36¾ inches by 25¾ inches by 34¾ inches overall. It can hold up to fifty Big Books upright in clear plastic sleeves with cardboard backing that come with the stand. The Big Book covers can be seen and flipped through like a giant book.

The traditional method for storing and displaying Big Books is to use 30 inch × 18 inch plastic hanging bags. These cost about $1.02 and up and you must purchase a rack to hang them on. A 36-inch-tall rack that holds fifty bags is $50.00 and up, depending on style. If you have a large collection, the cost can be prohibitive, as the bags tear and the plastic hangers break easily. The sturdiest bags available in a large size are 20 inches by 28 inches and are produced by Crystal Shield Bags. These are available from Demco (1-800-356-1200) for about $1.13 each.

A chart storage box is a cardboard storage box with large cardboard folders that can be labeled. The folders are 22⅝ inches by 23 inches. The cost is $40.00 for each box and set of folders. This method offers something a little nicer than the homemade container mentioned above. Chart boxes can be purchased from art-supply or library-supply catalogs.

Wall pockets are made to store Big Books. They are usually plastic and cost about $30.00. There are only three pockets on each one, and each pocket safely holds only about four books. The plastic is thin and tends to stretch especially around the metal grommets through which you attach the pocket to the wall. You can make your own wall pockets with grommets, from denim or canvas, but you must have plenty of empty wall space to use this as an effective storage tool.

Fiberboard portfolio cases are usually used for storing bulletin-board sets or posters. They are side opening with plastic carrying handles and measure 2¾ inches by 36 inches by 30 inches. You can buy six of them for $24.00 from art-supply houses. They are for storage only, and can be labeled. Each portfolio holds five to eight Big Books, fewer if you plan to transport them.

Big easels that are "made" to hold oversized books cost about $40.00 and up. Most are wood, but there are one or two wire easels available. Many of these "special" easels do not have a ledge wide enough to hold a Big Book as the pages are turned, and most are the wrong height and width for Big Book story sharing. The most economical and thoughtfully made of those available can be ordered from NASCO, 901 Janesville Avenue, P.O. Box 901, Fort Atkinson, WI, 53538-0901.

The ETA Primary Catalog (620 Lakeview Parkway, Vernon Hills, IL, 60061, 1-800-445-5985) is a source for two useful products to store and display your Big Books. Their economical, tabletop wire storage rack makes it easy to flip through Big Books. Each rack holds forty books upright. Cost is $29.95 ETA also has a maple easel with storage bars. This 42-inch easel has a 24-inch by 18-inch face. There is also a tray with two wooden pegs that hold the book open while allowing the pages to be turned. The storage bars on the back will hold eight books. The maple easel costs $59.95.

Circulating Big Books

Whether to circulate Big Books after you add them to your collection is a decision to be made on an individual basis. You must exercise care because of the generally flimsy construction of most Big Books. For example, special provisions must be made because Big Books cannot be returned in book drops—they are too fragile. Big Books are also easily damaged by children roughly turning the large pages, and even by them simply trying to transport them. A better choice is to have multiple copies of the book, or book and cassette, in regular-sized format available for circulation.

If you have teachers who wish to check out Big Books, or if your circulation policy is that you must circulate Big Books, the following precautions can help lengthen the shelf life of these items:

- Preserve your Big Books before they ever circulate. See the following information on preserving and repairing Big Books for preservation options.

- Circulate the books in some kind of protective covering to help prevent damage. This can be a plastic bag or cardboard folder, depending on how you decide to store and display your Big Books.

- Do not allow Big Books to be returned in the book drop.

Preserving and Repairing Big Books

Because of the fragile binding and construction of Big Books, you may have to invest a substantial amount of time on repairs and preventative maintenance on these items, especially if you circulate them. The following options will help make your Big Books less prone to damage.

Lamination

Some librarians choose to carefully remove the staples from the spine of a Big Book and laminate the entire book and its cover and then reassemble the book. This does make them last longer, but you run the risk of ruining part of the book if a heat laminator is used. Sometimes large items wrinkle in heat laminators with rollers. Cold lamination film is less easy to use and not cost effective, but there is a lower risk of ruining a page. Lamination film can also be expensive when each page of all of your Big Book collection is covered. A roll of 25 inches × 200 feet clear heat laminating film, lightweight, 1.5-mil. thick is about $17.00; while the 3- or 5-mil. is about $50.00. A roll of this film covers only about four books. This is a cost of $4.25 and $12.50 per book, respectively, if your library already owns a heat laminator. Cold lamination film is available in rolls of 4-mil. thick and 24 inches × 200 feet for $15.00. One roll would only cover eleven pages of Big Book. As you can see, cold lamination is very expensive.

Kapco Company Adhesive Products

This specialty company has a line of book-preservation products that work well to make Big Books sturdier. The unique nature of the adhesive products make it possible to preserve Big Books without going to the trouble of laminating each page. There are three products that can be used to make your Big Books shelf ready: Easy Cover, Easy Bind, and Easy Hold. Easy Cover is 5-mil. thick cold laminate book cover that comes in 25 inches × 25 yard rolls. Each roll will cover about fifty Big Book covers. Easy Bind is cold adhesive film that reinforces the cover to spine strength. A roll of 2 inches × 30 yards is $16.40 and will reinforce the spine strength on thirty books. Easy Hold are hour-glass-shaped strengtheners that hold pages of books to the spine. These are especially appropriate for the stapled bindings of Big Books. Easy Hold can be purchased for $0.11 each. The total cost of using the Kapco Products to strengthen your Big Books amounts to about $1.46 per book. Kapco products are available from Kent Adhesive Products, 930 Overholt Road, P.O. Box 626, Kent, OH, 44240, phone 1-800-791-8965.

Big Book Repair Kit

A repair kit is available from the Gaylord Company (1-800-448-6160). The kit includes shears, book tape, spine repair tape, and a bone folder. The cost is $40.00. This kit is adequate to repair Big Books that have been damaged and that you do not plan to circulate.

Sources of Big Book Equipment and Supplies

Demco
P.O. Box 7488
Madison, WI 53707-7488
(800) 356-1200
fax (800) 245-1329

ETA
620 Lakeview Parkway
Vernon Hills, IL 60061
(800) 445-5985
fax (800) ETA-9326

Gaylord
P.O. Box 4901
Syracuse, NY 13221-4901
(800) 448-6160
fax (800) 272-3412

Highsmith
W5527 Highway 106. P.O. Box 800
Fort Atkinson, WI 53538-0800
(800) 558-2110
fax (800) 835-2329

NASCO
901 Janesville Ave.
P.O. Box 901
Fort Atkinson, WI 53538-0901
(414) 563-2446
fax (414) 563-8296

Teaching Resource Center
P.O. Box 1509
San Leandro, CA 94577
(800) 833-3389
fax (800) 972-7722

Chapter 5

Using Big Books in Story Times and Programs

Big Books are designed to be shared with groups. The Big Books selected here are those that specifically appeal to children because of their language, repetition, rhyme, and predictability. These books also encourage participation and response by children by, for example, chiming in and repeating phrases and words. You can also elicit responses when you include activities in the story session that call for a child's participation. These activities can be art, drama, music, math, science, innovations on the text, or any other idea that relates to the concept or theme of the book. What follows here is a suggested list of activities that can be applied to any book, as well as some specific activities that work well with particular books. Some of the ideas here include fingerplays but for an especially good collection of fingerplays, songs, chants, and rhythms for Big Books, see *Warming Up to Big Books* by Cynthia Holley (The Wright Group, 1995).

General Ideas

Using any Big Book, elicit from the children further participation in the story by including these or similar tactics:

- Making a story cube for a particular Big Book by gluing child-designed pictures of the action in the text to a small square box. Roll the cube like a die and have children tell the part of the story that lands up.

- Pantomime favorite parts of a Big Book.

- Turn a favorite Big Book into a flannel story. Trace the story characters on non-woven fabric interfacing and color with colored pencils. "Prismacolor" pencils, available from art supply stores, work best on interfacing. Cut them out and have children retell the story by arranging the pieces on a board covered with heavy-duty flannel.

- Draw a mural of the setting of a favorite Big Book.

- Turn the characters from a Big Book into stick puppets. Trace them, color, and cut out. Tape to wooden dowels or craft sticks.

- Make bookmarks featuring favorite Big Book story characters.

- Trace pictures from a Big Book, color, and cut out. Use string to tie them to a coat hanger to create a story mobile.

- Create banners, pennants, charts, dioramas, lists, maps, quilts, puzzles, and greeting cards based on your favorite Big Book.

- Make a travel poster illustrative of the setting of a Big Book.

- Research scientific elements in Big Book stories, such as the weather, solar system, animals, and the like.

- Devise posters, book covers, and ads based on a Big Book.

- Big Book in a little bag: Photocopy the cover of a Big Book to fit the front of a grocery or shopping bag. Color the bag with crayons or markers. Glue the cover to the front of the bag. (If you laminate the cover, the bag will last longer.) Fill the bag with props and items related to the book featured. Present the bag to a group of children, and discuss or predict the story. Pull items from the bag and give hints or clues about the story to help them visualize the setting, characters, and so on. Now, share the Big Book!

- Patterns: Use any of the following ten patterns to respond to Big Books. Children can write sentences, illustrate, make books, write poems, or respond to stories in any other way they would like. Each pattern contains simple directions.

This doorhanger pattern can be drawn or written on about a Big Book. Hang on a doorknob and other places in your building to promote reading.

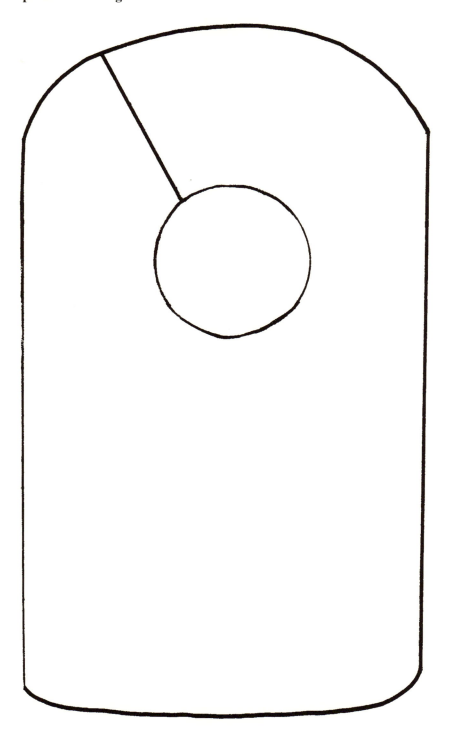

Title:

Recipe for: Book Title

Ingredients: Author, characters, setting, etc.

Directions: Plot

Story Cube: Write or draw on the sides of this cube. Cut out the pattern. Fold on the dotted lines and glue the sides together.

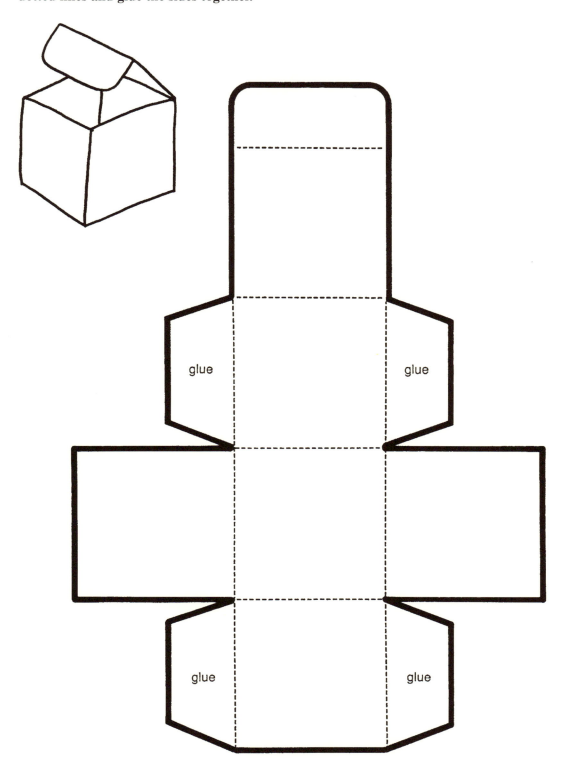

Decorate this visor with pictures from a Big Book. Cut out and stable to a paper strip that fits around the child's head.

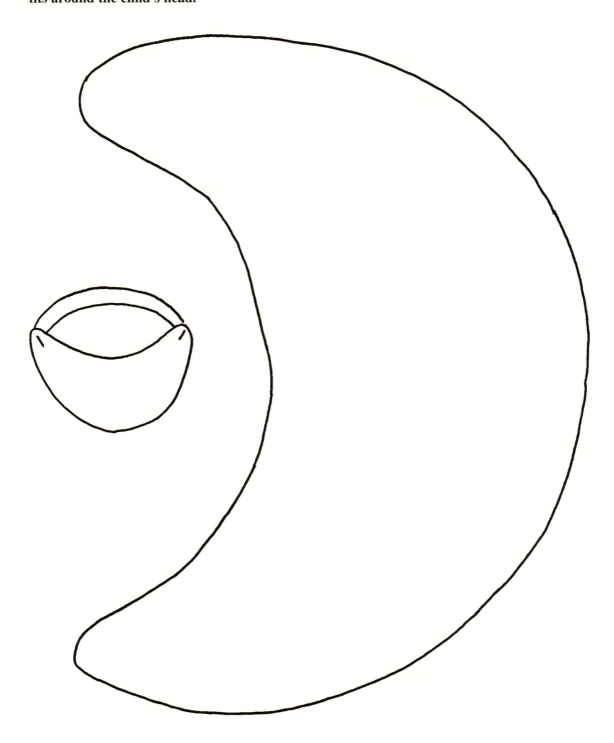

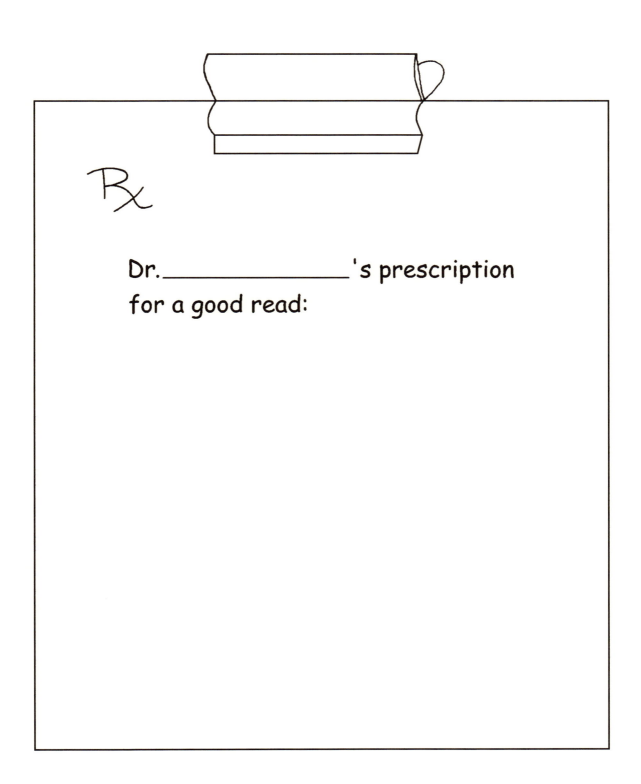

Ʀx

Dr._____'s prescription
for a good read:

Draw a picture and write the name of your favorite Big Book character or author on this stamp pattern.

Use this pattern for either a child's favorite Big Book character or for a shape book.

Book Award: Have the children write or draw a favorite Big Book title in the circle. Cut out and display on books.

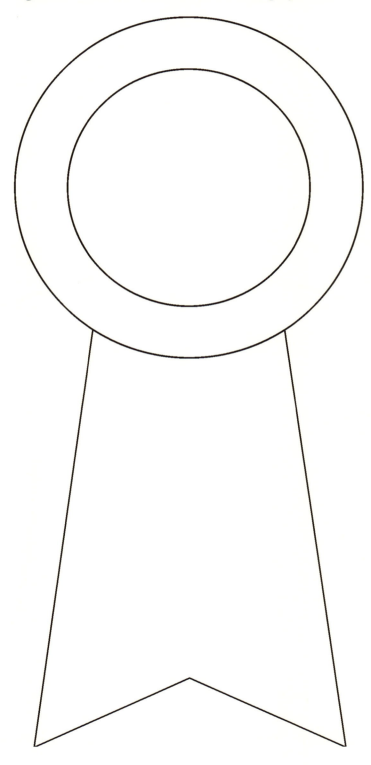

Specific Books

Beaver Tale by Lydia Dabcovich

Use the beaver pattern (p. 36) to make a beaver bulletin board. Research beavers and compare photographs from informational books to the illustrations in the Dabcovich book. Make a beaver dam out of craft paper and let each child add a beaver to the bulletin board.

Pretend to be busy beavers. Start by lying on the floor as if the beavers are sleeping. The children can act out the following movements as you recite them:

The beaver wakes up.
The beaver eats a big fish for breakfast.
The beaver chews on a tree.
The beaver carries a stick in his mouth.
The beaver takes a nap.
The beaver builds a dam of sticks.
The beaver hears a dog and runs away.
The beaver goes in the dam to sleep.

Can't You Sleep, Little Bear?
by Martin Waddell

Make a Little Bear that sits up. Reproduce the bear pattern (p. 37) on brown paper and cut it out. Laminate or cover with clear acetate. Fold on the dotted lines, and Little Bear will sit to listen to a story!

To make teddy bear paws from refrigerator biscuits, have each child use a dull knife to cut a biscuit into the shape of a bear paw. Brush each paw with melted margarine and sprinkle with cinnamon sugar. Bake according to package directions.

Corduroy by Donald Freeman

Corduroy puppets can be made using paper lunch sacks, crayons, scissors, glue, and the following patterns (pp. 38–39). Color the pattern and cut it out. Position the paper bag with the folded-over section facing up and the opening to the bottom. Glue the body on the lower part of the bag. Glue the head on the bag bottom, aligning with the body.

Use the bear tag patterns (p. 40) to make nametags for the puppets.

Curious George by H. A. Rey

These construction paper monkeys can hang from each other! Copy the pattern (p. 41) on brown paper and cut out. Let each child draw a "curious" face on their monkey and write his or her name on the back. Have one child hold a monkey, while the next one hangs a monkey on the first. Keep going and see how long your monkey chain becomes. These can also be attached to craft sticks and used with fingerplays about monkeys.

Dinosaurs, Dinosaurs by Byron Barton

Make a triceratops hat. For each child, you will need six 8-inch paper plates, scissors, stapler, hole punch, yarn, and whatever art materials you would like them to use to decorate (crayons, paint, markers, stickers, etc.). For the base of the hat, pinch a 2-inch by 4-inch section near the center of the paper plate with your fingers to form a raised hump, which will be a "snout." Cut another paper plate in half and tape one of the halves so that it stands up on the first paper plate to form a crest. Put it on the opposite end from the snout. Roll three paper plates into cones and staple to hold together. Tape them to the base, one on each side in front of the cone and one over the snout. Decorate the triceratops hat as desired. Punch a hole on each side of the hat and add yarn to tie on your head. Sing the song "If I Had a Dinosaur" by Raffi from the cassette *More Singable Songs* (MCA, 1977).

Fingerplay: "Good-bye, Dinosaurs"

Five enormous dinosaurs letting out a roar,
One is extinct and now there are four.
Four enormous dinosaurs munching on a tree,
One is extinct, and now there are three.
Three enormous dinosaurs, what can they do?
One is extinct, now there are two.
Two enormous dinosaurs, having fun,
One is extinct, now there is one.
One enormous dinosaur, blink, blink, blink.
Now he is gone, all are extinct.
(Hold up 5, 4, 3, 2, 1, and no fingers)

Song: "Dinosaurs Do"
(To the tune of "Ponchinella")

What can you do, brontosaurus, brontosaurus,
What can you do, brontosaurus funny you?
Oh I can eat a tree, brontosaurus,
    brontosaurus,
I can eat a tree, brontosaurus funny you!

Repeat with stegosaurus, poke my horn; pterodactyl, flap my wings, and the like.

Show the pictures from *Dinosaurs, Dinosaurs* of the different kinds of dinosaurs. Each child chooses a dinosaur to be. Play the music "Dinosaur" from the cassette *Monsters and Monstrous Things* by Jane Murphy (Kimbo, 1983). Have each child walk and make the noise that he or she thinks the chosen dinosaur would.

Where's the Dinosaur? Puppet

Materials for each puppet: Styrofoam cup, straw, green construction paper. You will also need: scissors, tape, copy of pattern.

Trace the dinosaur pattern (p. 42) onto the green paper and cut it out. Tape to the straw. Punch a hole in the bottom of the cup with

scissors, and insert the straw with the dinosaur through the hole. Hide the dinosaurs in the cup (they are extinct) and raise them up by pushing the straw up (they came back!).

The Doorbell Rang by Pat Hutchins

Make cookie pins. For each child, you will need one cookie, a paintbrush, diluted craft glue in a small container, glue, and a pin back. Each child will paint one side of a cookie with the diluted craft glue and paintbrush. When that side is dry, then turn it over and paint the reverse side. Repeat. When the cookies are completely dry, glue the pin backs on the bottom of the cookies. A good song to pair with this story is "Recipe" by Troubador from the cassette *Can We Grow?* (Gentle Wind, 1987). Organize a "Cookie Day," when children bring in their favorite cookies to share with the group. Conduct a taste test or dramatize the story with real cookies.

Each Orange Had 8 Slices by Paul Giganti

The narrator of this story visits many places, such as the school, zoo, and playground. Have the children reread the story carefully and list all the places he goes. Next have them draw a map of his journey. Illustrate the rest of the map to fill out an imaginary town.

Feathers For Lunch by Lois Ehlert

Make a pair of binoculars for bird watching. Each pair of binoculars requires two toilet paper rolls and a piece of string. Tape the two rolls together at the top and bottom. Use a hole punch to make holes on the top outside surfaces of each roll. Loop a string through these so the binoculars can be worn around the neck. Decorate the binoculars with crayons.

Fingerplay: "Five Birds"

Five birds up in a tree,
(Hold up five fingers)
A father, a mother,
(Hold up pointer, tall man)
And little birds three.
(Hold up other fingers)
One ate a bug,
One ate a worm,
One just sat and waited his turn.
(Hold up one, two, and three fingers)

Poetry: "A Bird Can Hear"

When a bird
Tilts her head
Sideways in
The flower bed,
She can hear
The tiny sound
Of a bug
Underground!

Make bird nests. You will need 6 tablespoons butter, 6 cups miniature marshmallows, 1 teaspoon vanilla, 1/2 teaspoon each of red and green food coloring, 8 cups of shredded wheat broken apart. Melt the margarine and the marshmallows together in a pan, stirring constantly. Remove from heat, add food coloring and vanilla. Fold in the shredded wheat. Cool, then let the children form into bird nests.

Freight Train by Donald Crews

Make a "Bottle Express" train! You will need 4 plastic bottles, such as bleach, detergent, or dish soap, in different sizes and colors; 16 plastic lids of various sizes; 4 aerosol spray caps; 1 35 mm film container; colored self-stick tape; 8 plastic straws; 16 nuts that will fit on straws; elastic cord; glue; and stickers. Remove the labels from the containers and wash the containers out thoroughly with soap. Using a sharp knife make two holes in the sides of each container and the center of each lid. Poke a straw through each of the holes in the container, putting two lids on one straw as if the lids were wheels. Secure the wheels to straws by gluing the nuts to the ends. Top each car with an aerosol can lid. For an engine, use a larger detergent bottle with the lid still on and use a film container to make the smokestack. Make windows from colored tape. To hook the train cars together, knot one end of a piece of elastic cord, poke a hole in the bottom of one container, tie to the lid of the next. Decorate with stickers.

Action Rhyme: "Train"

The train chugs slowly up the hill
And on the railroad track.
Clickety-clack, clickety clack,
Clickety-clack, clickety clack.
The train chugs faster up the hill
And on the railroad track.
Clickety-clack, clickety clack,
Clickety-clack, clickety clack.
The train chugs slower into town,
And on the railroad track.
Clickety-clack, clickety clack,
Clickety-clack, clickety clack.

Good Night, Owl! by Pat Hutchins

Reproduce or trace and cut out an owl pattern (p. 43) for each child. Instruct the children to trace around the owl's body on a piece of construction paper. This will be the cover of an "Owl Book." Then have them trace around the cover on several pieces of lined paper. These will be the pages of the book. Children can write stories or owl facts on the lined paper. Ideas for stories are "Who Are You?" with facts about owls, or a version of *Good Night, Owl!* called "Good Morning, Owl." Stack the pages and put the cover on top. Staple to the large owl pattern on the two "x" marks.

Growing Vegetable Soup by Lois Ehlert

Fingerplay: "Seeds"

These little seeds have a secret
(Cup hands)
I'll plant them all just so,
(Rake hands on palm)
And soon from inside themselves,
A plant will begin to grow!
(Slowly open fingers)

Poetry: "Little Seed"

Dig a little hole,
Plant a little seed,
Pour a little water—
Pull a little weed.
Chase away a bug,
Watch an April shower,
Have a little sunshine—
Grow a little flower.

Song: "Red Tomato Song"
(To the tune of "Little White Duck")

Big red tomato
Growing on the vine,

Big red tomato
I will make you mine.
You can make good food for me,
Soup, salad, pizza—Wheee!
Big red tomato,
Growing on the vine.

Make Sunflower Bread! For each loaf, you will need ¼ cup honey, ¼ cup butter, 2 beaten eggs, 1 cup whole wheat flour, 1 teaspoon salt, 1 tablespoon baking powder, 2 cups ground sunflower seeds (meat only), 1 cup milk. Beat together honey and butter, then add eggs. In another bowl, combine flour, baking powder, salt, and ½ the ground seeds and add half to honey mixture. Next add half the milk. Add the remaining honey mixture, mix, and add the remaining milk and mix. Fold in the rest of the seeds. Pour into a greased loaf pan and bake at 325 degrees for one hour. Cut when cooled.

Happy Birthday, Moon by Frank Asch

Make a moon mobile. Bend a wire hanger into a circle and bend the hook at the top to a right angle. Trace or copy the moon and star pattern (p. 44) onto paper and color as desired. Cut out the moon, stars, and bear and punch holes in them. Decorate the moon and stars with glitter. Attach to the hanger with thread.

Hattie and the Fox by Mem Fox

Use the patterns on pages 45–50 to do a modified reader's theater. Duplicate the patterns so that the number of each pattern is even and you have enough for each child to receive one. Cut out the patterns and pass out randomly. The animal a child receives represents the child's group. Divide the groups into

"Hatties" cows, pigs, geese, sheep, and horses. Each group will say the appropriate animal's words during a retelling of the story.

A House Is a House for Me
by Mary Ann Hobermann

Give a copy of the house pattern (p. 51) to each child to decorate the front and back. Then have the child draw a picture of his or her family on the reverse side. Fold the houses and display.

How Much Is a Million?
by David Schwartz

Make magician puppets to help tell the story. For each child, you will need a magician hat pattern (p. 52), a 12-inch square of black fabric, a 2½-half inch styrofoam ball with a hole on one side, a cotton ball, glue, scissors, 1 half sheet of black construction paper, gummed-back gold and silver stars, 2 wiggle eyes, and a marker. Use the hat pattern to cut a hat from black construction paper. Decorate it with gummed stars. Decorate one side of the black fabric with stars also. Glue the hat on top of the Styrofoam ball, on the opposite side of the hole. The ball is the wizard's head. Draw a face on the ball with the marker. Stretch out the cotton ball and glue it to the foam ball as a beard. Place the fabric over the child's hand and put the child's finger in the hole in the Styrofoam ball.

I Like Me! by Nancy Carlstrom

On the last page of this story, Louanne Pig is wearing a cheerful, heart-shaped badge. Provide paper, scissors, and crayons for the children to create their own badges.

I Love Cats by Catherine Matthias

There are many different pictures of cats in this story. Discuss different breeds of cats and show pictures from factual books. Copy and pass out the cat pattern (p. 53). Let each child choose a favorite cat and color their copy to resemble it.

Play the game "Mother Cat and Kittens": One child is the mother cat. She sleeps and the other children, who are the kittens, hide in the area. The mother cat hunts the kittens and returns them to a "home" chair.

Rhyme: Mother Cat

Mother cat and kittens
Fast asleep one day—
But kittens got up quietly
And tiptoed away.

In the Tall, Tall Grass
by Denise Fleming

Make paper ladybugs (see p. 54). Each child will need a 5-inch square of red or yellow paper, a black crayon, and scissors. You will also need a tree branch and glue. Have the child select red or yellow paper. Fold the paper diagonally in half. Fold the resulting triangle to make a small square as shown. Hold the folded end of the square and round off the open end as shown. Add black dots to the ladybugs with the crayons. Display the completed ladybugs by gluing them to a tree branch.

Fingerplay: "Firefly"

1, 2, 3, 4, 5,
(Open up each finger on left hand)
I caught a firefly alive!

6, 7, 8, 9, 10,
(Open up each finger on right hand)
I let it go again.
(Throw arms in the air)

Fingerplay: "Little Turtle"

I have a little turtle,
(Hold hands together to form small circle)
He lives in a box.
(Put right hand flat over left hand)
He swims in the water,
(Make swimming motion)
He climbs on the rocks.
(Make climbing motion)
He snapped a mosquito,
He snapped a flea,
He snapped a minnow,
And he snapped at me.
(Clap each time you say "snap")
He caught the mosquito,
He caught the flea,
He caught the minnow,
(Make catching motion each time you say
   "caught")
But he didn't catch me!
(Point to self and shake head no)

Song: "Catch a Firefly"
(To the tune of "London Bridge")

Catch a firefly, let it go,
Let it go, let it go,
Catch a firefly, let it go,
Bye, bye firefly!

"Ladybug" (Make up a tune)

Ladybug, ladybug, fly away home!
Your house is on fire and your kids are alone!
Ladybug, ladybug, come back today,
The fire is out and your kids are okay.

Hold a Bug Bash! Pass out the InSacks described below. Play a simple version of "Duck, Duck, Goose," but call it "Spider, Spider, Fly." Serve "Grasshopper Punch" (apple juice with green food coloring added).

To make InSacks you will need for each child:

1 large paper sack, half a piece of red posterboard, 2 black pipe cleaners or chenille stems. You will also need a black marker, scissors, glue, and an enlarged copy of the ladybug pattern (p. 55).

Trace the pattern on the posterboard. Outline all black lines and color the ladybugs pupils black with the marker. Add some nice ladybug dots. Cut the ladybug out and glue to the back of the sack, slipping the pipe cleaners under the head as antennae. Cut off the bottom of the sack and cut out two circles, one on each side, to serve as arm holes. The sack slips over the child's head.

It Looked Like Spilt Milk
by Charles G. Shaw

Make cotton clouds with cotton balls, crayons, construction paper, and glue. Tell the children to draw a scene on the paper, leaving plenty of sky. Glue cotton in the sky area to resemble differently shaped clouds

The Itsy Bitsy Spider by Iza Trapani

Create a spider vivarium, which is a habitat in which they can live. You will need sterile potting soil, a small aquarium, leaves, rocks, a branch, a small wet sponge, cheesecloth, and tape. Place the soil in the bottom of the aquarium. Cover the soil with leaves, rocks, and branches. Place a wet sponge in the tank for moisture. Place a captured or purchased spider in the tank. Cover the top with cheesecloth and tape shut. Feed the spider live insects. After observing for a while, set the spider free in a park.

Jump, Frog, Jump! by Robert Kalan

Make jumping frogs for each child. Materials: frog pattern (p. 56), reproduced for each participant on light green paper; 10 lily pads, reproduced on dark green paper, numbered 0 through 9; 4-inch sections of straight plastic straws, one for each participant; one flexible plastic straw for each participant that must be a slightly larger diameter than the straight straws; transparent tape; masking tape; and a ruler.

Each child writes his or her name on a frog. Using masking tape, tape the lily pads to the floor, placing them in a line 1 foot apart. Each child folds the top of their straight straw section down about 1 inch and tape the folded end to the back of their frog. Each child will now insert the free end of the straight straw into the shorter end of the flexible straw. Then each child in turn will then stand behind the lily pad numbered zero and blow through the open end of the flexible straw to launch the frog in a giant jump.

Little Nino's Pizzeria by Karen Barbour

Make your own pizzeria! Do any of the following pizza-related activities after sharing the book.

Sing the "Pizza Song" to the tune of "Twinkle, Twinkle, Little Star":

Pizza, pizza. It's a treat.
Pizza pie is fun to eat.

Ooey, gooey cheese so yummy,
Crunchy crust goes in my tummy.
Pizza, pizza. It's a treat.
Pizza pie is fun to eat.

Accompany this song with rhythm band featuring some instruments that "really cook," such as spoons, rolling pins, pans, and the like. Encourage kids to be creative about the way they "play" their instruments.

Make paper pizzas! Use the pizza patterns (p. 57) provided to decorate a brown paper circle to look like a pizza. Laminate the completed pizzas, and then cut apart to make pizza puzzles. Store pizza puzzles in an empty pizza box. Discuss with children what made *Little Nino's Pizzeria* and Little Tony's pizza from the story special. Talk about the children's favorite types of pizza, and unusual pizza that you might not ever see, such as pickle pizza. Encourage kids to draw their favorites.

The Little Old Woman and the Hungry Cat by Nancy Polette

Make hungry cats to stuff full. Trace the illustration of the cat on page 18 of the Big Book to use as a pattern. Each child needs two of these patterns reproduced on construction paper. Cut out the two patterns and lay one on top of the other, lining up the edges. Staple the two patterns together, but leave a 2-inch opening unstapled. Through this opening, stuff the cats with cotton balls. Staple the opening closed. Kids can color their hungry cats with crayons.

Little Red Hen by Byron Barton

Use the patterns from pages 48, 50, and 58–60 to make stick puppets and have the children retell *Little Red Hen*. Use the Hen Sack Puppet patterns to make red hens for each child out of paper sacks to decorate and take home.

Madeline by Ludwig Bemelmans

Learn "Happy Birthday" in French.

Bonne anniversaire a toi,
(Bunn ah-nee-vaire-saire ah twah)
Bonne anniversaire a toi,
(Bunn ah-nee-vaire-saire ah twah)
Bonne anniversaire, cher Madeline,
(Bunn ah-nee-vaire-saire sher Madeline)
Bonne anniversaire a toi.
(Bunn ah-nee-vaire-saire ah twah)

Make a Madeline hinged hat. Each child will need a 9-inch paper plate and a pair of scissors. You will also need materials to decorate the hat, such as paper flowers, ribbon, feathers, and the like. Cut out the center of the plate, leaving it attached with a 2-inch hinge. Bend the cut piece down so that it sits at the back of your head. Each child then decorates as desired.

The Milk Makers by Gail Gibbons

Use the cow pattern (p. 46). Reproduce the pattern onto stiff white paper, one for each child. Let the kids color the cows as they like. Tape small, slightly inflated balloons to the back of the cut out cows near the stomach area to serve as udders.

The Mitten by Jan Brett

Children participate in retelling the story by creating masks for the animals in the book.

If you have a large group, extra children can be the sneeze, saying "Aaaachoo!" at the appropriate moment. A white knitted shawl or blanket can wrap around the children as the mitten.

Mouse Paint by Ellen W. Stoll

Give each child a sign to wear around the neck. The signs must either be in primary (red, yellow, or blue) or secondary (orange, green, or purple) colors. As each color is named in the story, the children who are wearing that color stand up. As the story ends, the children will sit down when they hear their color named again.

Sing the song "Mixing Colors" by Gary Rosen from the cassette *Tot Rock* (Lightyear Music, 1993) after sharing the book.

My Five Senses by Aliki

You can assemble Smell Plates using paper plates, assorted "smelly" items such as cloves, bay leaves, mint, or perfumed cotton and glue. The children should write "My Smell Plate" and their name on their paper plates. They can then arrange and glue smelly items to the plate.

On the Day You Were Born by Debra Frazier

Create a slide book by making one copy of the Earth pattern (p. 61) for each child. Have them color and cut out the Earth. This will be the cover of the slide book. Cut about ten sheets of blank paper to fit the size of the cover. Attach them to the cover using a brass fastener. Encourage the children to write or draw in their slide book.

Over the River and through the Wood by Lydia Maria Child

Using the illustrations in the story as a guide, create a winter scene that includes Grandmother's house. Cover a card table with cotton batting. Make houses from milk cartons or Popsicle sticks. Use a mirror to represent water or a lake. Paper figures can be drawn on paper, cut out, and taped to chenille stems so they will stand up. Encourage the children to think of imaginative ways to create their village snow scene.

Paul Bunyan by Steven Kellogg

Make Paul Bunyan sack puppets using the patterns on p. 62 and lunch sacks. Color the patterns and cut out. Glue the head part to the flat bottom of the lunch sack and glue the mouth underneath the flap.

Write your own tall tales. You will need a roll of adding machine or cash register paper and a copy of the pattern. Children sit in a long line facing the same direction, toward the top of the paper roll. Unroll the paper in front of them. Each child adds a tall tale sentence to the paper, building on the sentence of the child in front of them. A child may also go to the end of the line and add another sentence if desired. Cut out a copy of the pattern on p. 63 and glue to the top and bottom of your very own tall tale. Display on a long, long wall!

Peanut Butter and Jelly by Nadine Wescott

Ask the children what they think peanut seeds need in order to grow into plants. Make a chart of their responses. (Plants need soil, sun, and water.) Have each child prepare a raw, shelled peanut for planting by soaking it overnight in a Styrofoam cup of water. Explain that water softens up the food stored in the peanut until the food breaks into tiny bits. This helps the plant begin to grow. The following day, have the children take out the peanuts, empty the water, and fill the cups three-quarters full of soil. Show them how to press the seeds about 1 inch down into the soil. Set the cups in a warm, sunny place and keep the soil moist. Within a week to ten days the first green sprouts will appear.

Planting a Rainbow by Lois Ehlert

Make a flower press. Children will need two 12 inches × 15 inches × ¼ inch plywood squares, corrugated cardboard cut to the same size, paper towels, old belts to use as straps, and flower specimens. Layer the plywood, cardboard (with the corrugations perpendicular to the 15-inch side of the plywood), two paper towels, flower specimens, two more paper towels, and another piece of cardboard. Continue to alternate cardboard, paper towels, and flowers, ending with the plywood. A single press will hold about thirty cardboard and paper towel sandwiches. Have a child stand on the press and secure the belts tightly around it. Tighten the straps every few days and leave until dry.

Make a group rainbow book. Trace or reproduce the rainbow pattern (p. 64) on white posterboard. This will be the cover. Trace or reproduce and cut out one rainbow pattern for each child using various colors of paper. Have each child write a favorite color or flower poem on the page. Gather the stacks of paper together and place the cover on the top. Punch two holes on the left side of the cover. Lace an 18-inch piece of rainbow yarn through the bottom hole from the back and secure the end with a piece of tape. Pull the yarn through the top hole toward the inside of the book. Punch a hole in each page in various places and pull the yarn through each hole, leaving plenty of slack for turning the pages. On the last page, lace the yarn through the hole and secure on the back of the book with a piece of tape. The book will stand up for display.

The Rainbow Fish by Marcus Pfister

Decorate the area in which you will share the book with blue streamers and multicolored paper fish to simulate an underwater environment. Serve fish-shaped crackers. Set up a small aquarium for the kids to observe.

Fingerplay: "Five Fish"

Five little fish swam by the shore,
One ate a worm and then there were four.
Four little fish swam in the sea,
One blew a bubble and then there were three.
Three little fish swam in the blue,
One hid in seaweed and then there were two.
Two little fish swam in the sun,
One met a clam and then there was one.
One little fish, splash, splash, splash.
He went home in a flash, flash, flash.

Make a paper plate fish (see p. 65). Cut a triangular shape out of one edge of a paper plate. Have the children glue the triangle to the plate on the side opposite where you cut. The cut is the mouth and the triangle is the tail.

Have each child think of a characteristic that would make a fish special or unusual. Let them decorate their paper-plate fish to be their special fish.

The Snowy Day by Ezra Jack Keats

Cut simple snowflakes from white paper (see p. 66). Attach the snowflakes to thread and tape to straws. Pass one out to each child. The straw is used as a handle to hold the threaded snowflake. Have the children blow the snowflake to make it fall, twirl, and spin.

Strega Nona by Tomie De Paola

Cut paper in the shape of Strega Nona's pasta pot. The children can write or dictate a story about what recipe they would cook using a magic pot.

Ten Little Mice by Joyce Dunbar

Make mouse bookmarks from felt. You will need felt or flannel scraps, yarn scraps, pipe cleaners, glue, scissors, and string. Trace the pattern (p. 67) for the mouse's body onto one color felt. Cut slits in the body through which to put the ear piece. Use a contrasting color of felt to trace and cut the ear piece. Put the ears through the body. Glue on eyes cut from scraps, or use wiggly eyes available at craft stores. Glue on yarn for a tail. Glue on string for whiskers. Attach the back of the slit part to a pipe cleaner to make a bookmark.

Thump, Thump, Rat-a-Tat-Tat by Gene Baer

As you share the book, have the children clap to the rhythms of the story, softer and louder as appropriate

Tommy at the Grocery Store
by Bill Grossman

Make pig snouts so the kids can pretend to be Tommy. You will need cardboard egg cartons (flat bottomed), scissors, felt-tip pens, large rubber bands, stapler. Cut the egg cartons apart into individual egg cups and give one to each child. Use the markers to color the egg holders pink. These are the pig snouts. Add nostrils with a black marker. Staple a rubber band to the sides of the snout to hold the snout in place around a child's head.

Another fun activity is to use the pattern (p. 68) to make pigs with pink, round balloons. Draw the eyes and mouth on a balloon with a marker. Copy the patterns onto pink paper, cut out, and tape to the balloon as shown.

The Very Hungry Caterpillar
by Eric Carle

After sharing the Big Book, let each child decorate a butterfly pattern (p. 69) with crayons, glitter, and sequins. Hang with string from the ceiling to create a butterfly "flock."

Where Does the Brown Bear Go?
by Nicki Weiss

Use the pattern (p. 70) to make brown bear necklaces. Trace or copy onto brown

paper and cut out. Punch a hole in each bear and reinforce with tape around the hole to avoid tearing. String the bears on yarn.

Who Is the Beast? by Keith Baker

Reproduce one copy of the tiger pattern (p. 71) for each child. Color the tigers yellow or orange as desired. Give each child some black yarn and glue. Glue one end of the yarn to the rear of the tiger, then glue down the rest of the yarn in a wavy stripe to the shoulder.

Who Lost a Shoe? by Barbara Hazen

Duplicate a supply of the shoe pattern (p. 72) onto posterboard so that there are enough for each child to receive one. Cut out each shoe shape, and punch holes in the cutouts where the laces go. Lace each shoe with a length of yarn. The children can practice tying their own special shoe.

Why Can't I Fly?
by Rita Golden Gelman

Dramatize this story. Characters needed are Minnie the monkey, bluebird, ladybug, yellow bird, duck, and a butterfly. Use boots, blue feathers, yellow feathers, black paper spots, and paper duck and butterfly wings as props to designate each character.

Use with *Beaver Tail*.

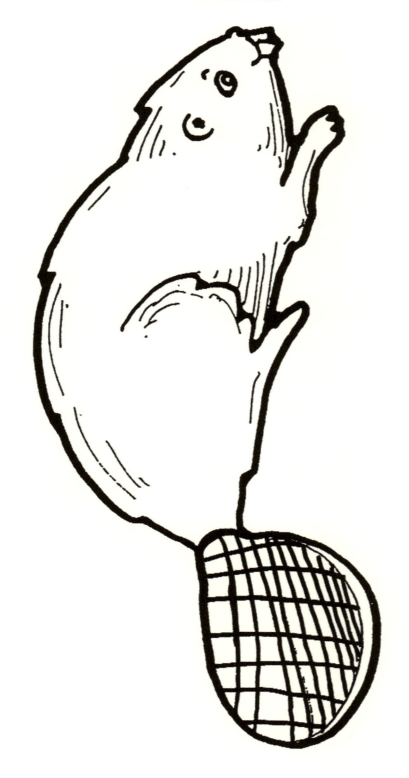

Corduroy Puppet: Use with *Corduroy*.

Corduroy Puppet: Use with *Corduroy*.

Bear Tags: Use with *Corduroy*.

Monkey: Use with *Curious George*.

Use with *Dinosaurs, Dinosaurs*.

Mobile Pattern: Use with *Happy Birthday, Moon*.

Hen: Use with *Hattie and the Fox*.

Cow: Use with *Hattie and the Fox* and *The Milk Makers*.

Sheep: Use with *Hattie and the Fox*.

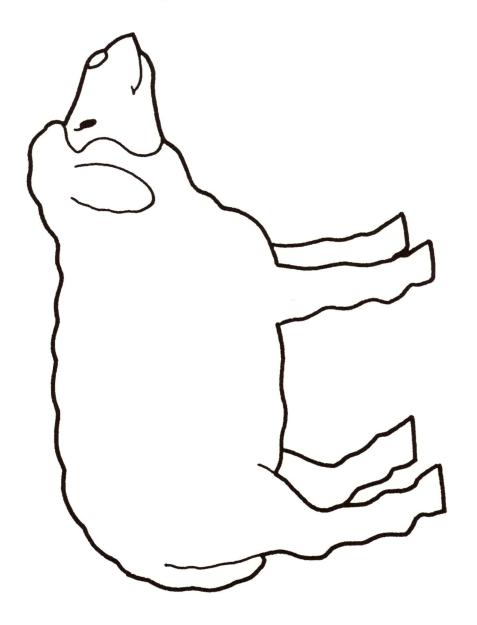

Pig: Use with *Hattie and the Fox* and *Little Red Hen*.

Horse: Use with *Hattie and the Fox*.

Goose: Use with *Hattie and the Fox* and *Little Red Hen*.

House: Use with *A House Is a House for Me*.

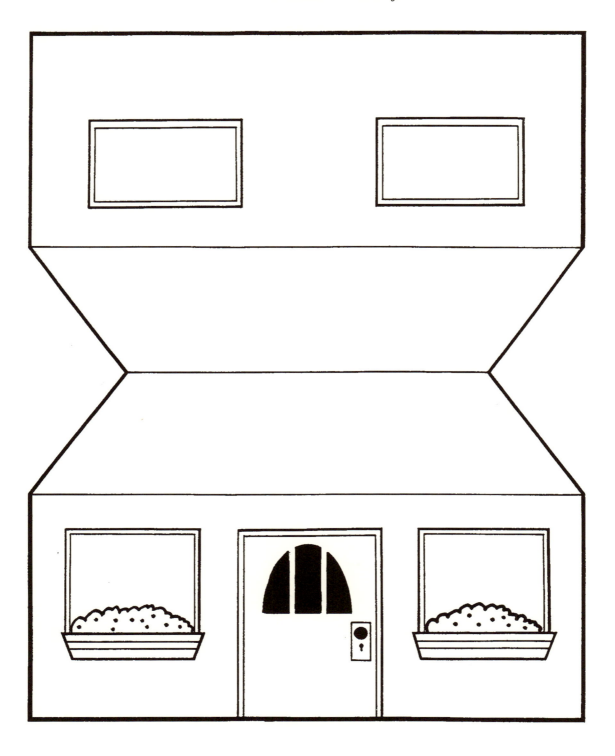

Magician Hat Pattern: Use with *How Much Is a Million?*

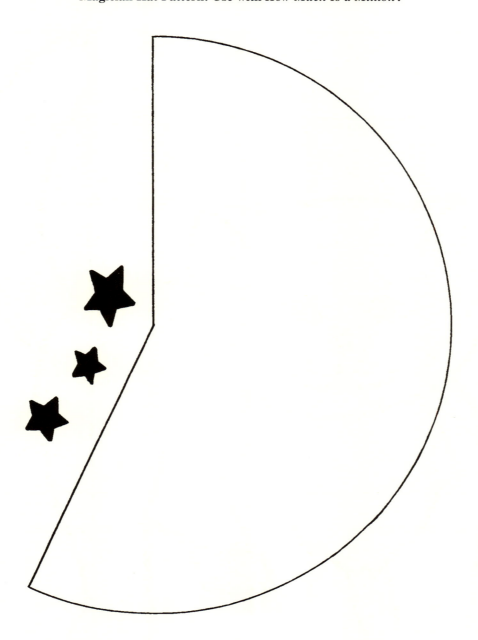

Origami Ladybug: Use with *In the Tall, Tall Grass*.

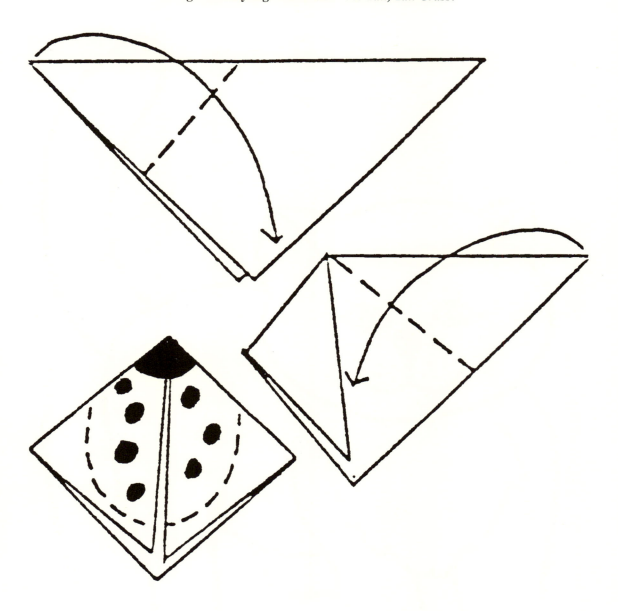

InSack Pattern: Use with *In the Tall, Tall Grass*.

Pizza-topping Patterns: Use with *Little Nino's Pizzeria*.

Cat: Use with *Little Red Hen*.

Hen Sack Puppet: Use with *Little Red Hen*.

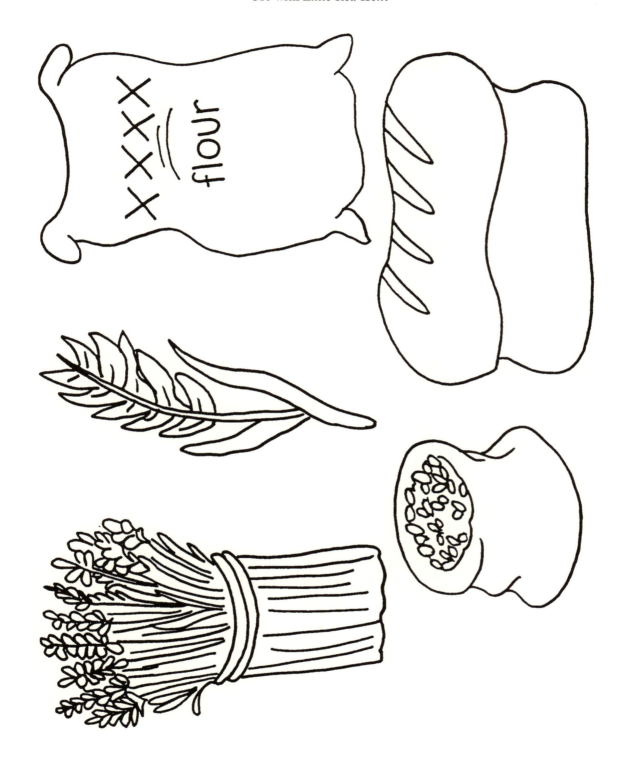

Slide Book Pattern: Use with *On the Day You Were Born*.

Paul Bunyan Sack Puppet: Use with *Paul Bunyan*.

Dancing Snowflake: Use with *The Snowy Day*.

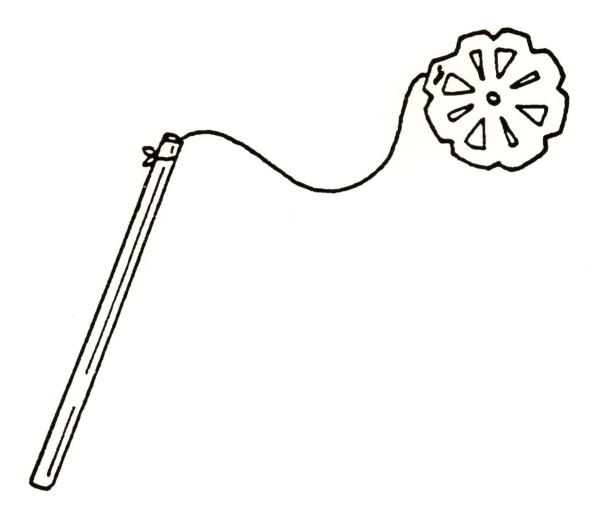

Mouse: Use with *Ten Little Mice*.

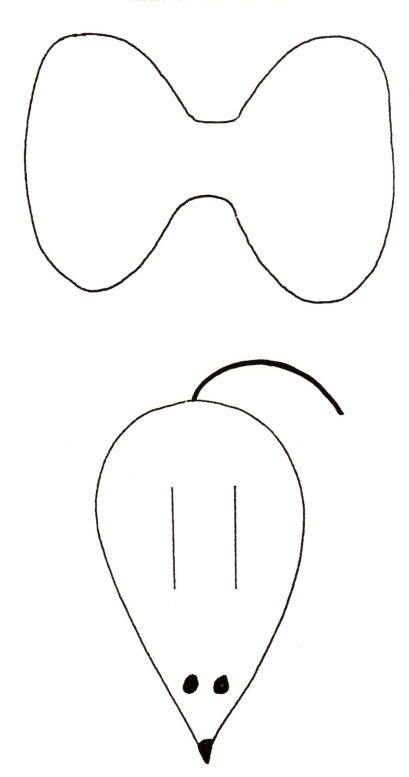

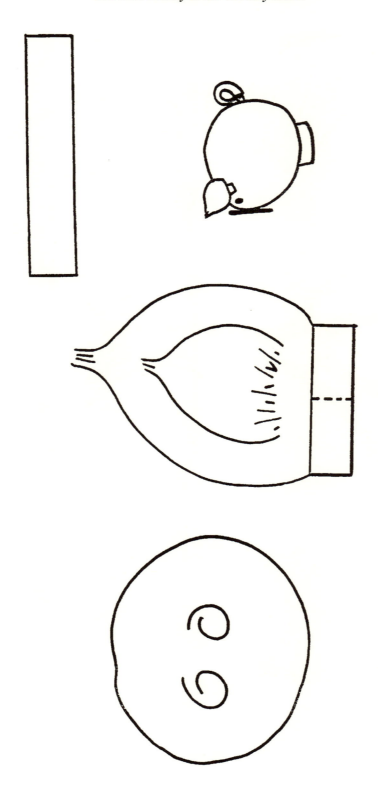

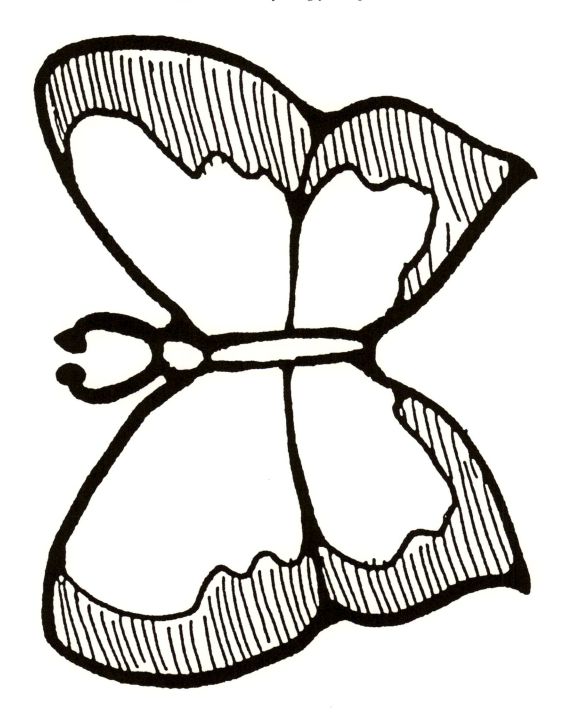

Tiger: Use with *Who Is the Beast?*

Shoe: Use with *Who Lost a Shoe?*

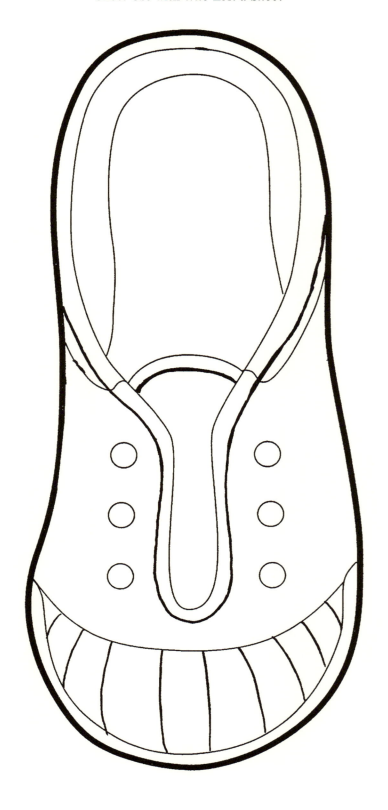

Chapter 6

Conclusion and Selected Bibliography

Big Books allow children to play the role of successful readers even before they learn to read! The use of Big Books provides motivation through the feeling of accomplishment that accompanies shared reading experiences. Children want to learn to read because they have experienced that they can read through these books. They enjoy the large, bright pictures, the metered text, and high interest plots of selected Big Books. For further reading on Big Books, see the following resources.

Selected Bibliography

Barret, F. L. *A Teacher's Guide to Shared Reading*. Scholastic-TAB, 1982.

"Big Books." *School Librarian's Workshop* (April 1996): 9.

Bullock, Charles, and Catherine Bullock. *A Little Book about Big Books*. Link Learning, 1987.

Carter, Betty. "Fall Roundup." *Book Links* (November 1994): 58–60.

———. "Big Books." *Book Links* (November 1995): 59–62.

Carter, Betty, and James L. Thomas. "Big Books: Purchasing and Using Enlarged Texts." *Book Links* (November 1991): 15–17.

Cowley, Joy. "Joy of Big Books." *Instructor* (October 1991): 19.

Cullinan, Bernice, and Carolyn Carmichael. *Literature and Young Children*. National Council of Teachers of English, 1977.

Cutting, Brian. *Getting Started in Whole Language*. The Wright Group, 1990.

Davidson, Merylin, and Ritya Isherwood. *Moving On with Big Books*. Scholastic, 1991.

Donahue, Richard. "Books Big and Small." *Publishers Weekly* (February 12, 1992): 13–15.

Fisher, Bobbi. *Joyful Learning*. Heinemann, 1991.

Friedland, Jeni. "The Big Book Buying Guide." *Instructor* (October 1991): 22.

Hamilton, Martha, and Mitch Weiss. *Children Tell Stories: A Teaching Guide*. Richard C. Owen, 1990.

Holdaway, Don. *The Foundations of Literacy*. Ashton Scholastic, 1979.

Holley, Cynthia. *Warming Up to Big Books*. The Wright Group, 1995.

Irwin, Christine. "Small Children Fall for Big Books." *Instructor* (October 1991): 21.

Lynch, Priscilla. *Using Big Books and Predictable Books*. Scholastic, 1986.

Park, B. "The Big Book Trend: A Discussion with Don Holdaway." *Language Arts* 59 (1982): 815–821.

Reed, Vicky. "Big Books for Big Kids." *Instructor* (October 1991): 20.

Scholastic Staff. *Big Books: Practical Strategies*. (Video, 15 minutes). Scholastic Inc., 1996.

Slaughter, Judith. "Big Books for Little Kids: Another Fad or a New Approach for Teaching Beginning Reading?" *The Reading Teacher* (April 1983): 758–762.

———. *Beyond Storybooks*. DRA, 1994.

Strickland, Dorothy. "Some Tips for Using Big Books." *The Reading Teacher* (May 1988): 966–968.

Strickland, Dorothy, and Lesley Morrow. *Emerging Literacy: Young Children Learn to Read and Write*. International Reading Association, 1989.

———. "Sharing Big Books." *The Reading Teacher* (January 1990): 342–343.

Watson-Newlin, Karen L. "Big Books." *School Arts* (February 1990): 42–43.

Chapter 7

Annotated Bibliography of Recommended Big Books with Age Levels

The following is a list of Big Books for school and public libraries. These books are considered auxiliary library materials for most libraries. The books in this list were chosen for their child appeal of story and pictures. Also taken into consideration were literary merit and characteristics such as repetition, cumulative sequence, rhythm, rhyme, and predictability. Technically, the Big Book must replicate the smaller version of the book, if one exists. This means that there must be clear, proportionate illustrations with the same colors and amount of detail. Text should also be in the same font and words in the same place on the page as the smaller version. Quality of construction and binding were also considered. If a book is not a primary purchase, the annotation indicates the reason.

Aardema, Verna. *Bringing the Rain to Kapiti Plain*. Scholastic, 1994. 14" × 18", $24.95, Gr 2–3. Rhyming African folktale about how Ki-pat brings the rain to Kapiti Plain.

———. *Why Mosquitoes Buzz in People's Ears*. Puffin/Pied Piper, 1975. 13½" × 17", $17.99, Ps–Gr 3. Cumulative retelling of a West African tale that includes repeated phrases and word sounds for joining in.

Ahlberg, Janet, and Allan Ahlberg. *Each Peach Pear Plum*. Puffin, 1986. 15" × 19", $24.95, Ps. Children can play "I Spy" with characters hiding in the pictures of this rhymed text.

Alborough, Jez. *Where's My Teddy?* Candlewick, 1992. 14⅞" × 18", $19.99, Ps. When a boy named Eddie goes looking for his lost teddy bear in the woods, he comes across a large bear with a similar problem.

Aliki. *My Five Senses*. HarperCollins, 1989. 15¼" × 18½", $19.95, Gr 2. Let's Read and Find Out About Science Series. The text encourages interaction as the senses are introduced through a guessing game. Shows what the senses are and how we use them.

———. *My Visit to the Dinosaurs*. HarperCollins, 1994. 16½" × 12¾", $19.95, Gr 2. During his visit to a natural history museum, a boy finds out all about dinosaurs. An excellent introduction to paleontology.

Andriani, Vincent. *Peanut Butter Rhino*. Scholastic, 1994. 15" × 19", $19.95, Gr K. A rhinoceros searches through the jungle for the peanut butter sandwich he lost from his lunch box. This very short book is not a primary purchase.

Anholt, Catherine, and Laurence Anholt. *All About You*. Scholastic, 1994. 15" × 19", $24.95, Ps. A rhyming book that encourages kids to talk about themselves and their daily rituals.

Anno, Mitsumasa. *Anno's Counting Book*. Crowell, 1992. 17" × 15", $19.95, Gr K–3. An introduction to number systems through a wordless picture book in which a town is shown growing up over the course of a year.

Appelt, Kathi. *Elephants Aloft*. HBJ, 1994. 16⅜" × 18", $20.00, Ps. Two elephants take off from India in a hot air balloon that is bound for Africa. Story features use of prepositions.

Armajo, Charlotte. *Desert Dance*. Celebration Press, 1995. 14" × 18", $20.00, Ps. Various animals of the desert dance under the harvest moon.

Arnold, Ted. *No Jumping on the Bed*. Scholastic, 1987. 15" × 19", $24.95, Ps. A boy embarks on an exciting nighttime adventure as he crashes through the floors of his building and meets a succession of neighbors.

Asch, Frank. *Bear Shadow*. Scholastic, 1988. 18" × 24", $24.95, Gr K–1. A gentle bear is confused by his own shadow.

———. *Bear's Bargain*. Scholastic, 1992. 18" × 24", $24.95, Gr K–1. Two friends find clever, creative ways to make each other's wishes come true.

———. *Happy Birthday, Moon*. Modern Curriculum Press, 1986. 18" × 24", $49.95, Ps. Bear cannot decide what gift to buy the moon for its birthday until he sees the perfect gift in the hat shop. Please note the cost of the book is higher because it is hardbound.

———. *Here Comes the Cat*. Scholastic, 1987. 18" × 24", $19.95. Ps. A mouse rides a bicycle, boat, plane, and fish in order to evade a cat.

———. *Mooncake*. Scholastic, 1986. 18" × 24", $24.95, Gr K–1. A gentle bear decides that he would like to taste the moon, and he does!

———. *Moondance*. Scholastic, 1993. 18" × 24", $24.95, Gr K–1. This book tells the simple story of bear's wish to dance with the moon.

———. *Moongame*. Scholastic, 1992. 18" × 24", $24.95, Gr K–1. Bear plays hide-and-seek with the moon.

Avery, Kristin. *The Crazy Quilt*. Celebration Press, 1995. 14" × 18", $20.00, Ps. A mother and child bear make a quilt using old clothes that hold memories for them.

Aylesworth, Jim. *Old Black Fly*. Henry Holt, 1992. 15" × 17", $18.95, Gr 1–3. Rhyming text and illustrations follow a mischievous old black fly all through the alphabet as he has a very busy, bad day landing where he should not be.

Bacon, Ron. *Wind*. Scholastic, 1989. 17⅞" × 14½", $24.95, Gr K–1. Rhythmic and gentle text elicit the whispery feel of the wind.

Baer, Gene. *This Is the Way We Go to School*. Scholastic, 1992. 15½" × 18½", $24.95, Gr K–2. Rhyming text tells how children around the world get to school.

———. *Thump, Thump, Rat-a-Tat-Tat*. HarperCollins, 1989. 15" × 17½", $19.95, Ps. The sounds of a marching band get louder and softer in this colorful book of rhythmic refrains.

Baker, James. *Who Is the Beast?* HBJ, 1990. 15" × 17", $20.00, Ps. Lavish illustrations depict a bee, snake, frog, catfish, and monkey who all chatter about a frightening beast—a tiger.

Baker, Jeannie. *Where the Forest Meets the Sea*. Scholastic, 1987, 15" × 18", $19.95, Gr 1–3. Fabric and collage illustrations depict the story of a boy and his father who are shadowed by the memories of extinct animals and plants on a deserted island.

Bang, Molly. *Ten, Nine, Eight*. Scholastic, 1983. 18" × 18", $18.95, Ps. Familiar bedtime objects are counted in this gentle good-night story featuring a father and daughter.

Barbour, Karen. *Little Nino's Pizzeria*. HBJ, 1991. 17" × 18", $19.95, Gr 1–3. Tony likes to help his father in their small family restaurant until it becomes a fancier place.

Barrett, Judi. *Animals Should Definitely Not Wear Clothing*. Simon and Schuster, 1988. 14½" × 18½", $24.95, Ps–Gr 1. Funny illustrations depict the absurdity of clothing on animals.

Barton, Byron. *Dinosaurs, Dinosaurs*. Harper-Collins, 1989. 14½" × 17", $19.95, Ps–Gr 1. In prehistoric days, there were many kinds of dinosaurs—big, small, those with spikes and sharp teeth.

———. *Little Red Hen*. HarperCollins, 1993. 17½" × 17½", $19.95, Ps. Traditional tale of the animals refusal to help the hen do the work and get no reward in the end.

———. *The Three Bears*. HarperCollins, 1994. 18" × 18", $19.95, Ps. Bold and brightly colored flat paintings illustrate this basic retelling that has a few rhythmic refrains.

Bayer, Jane. *A, My Name Is Alice*. Puffin, 1994. 17⅞" × 15", $18.99, Gr 1–3. An alphabet jump-rope rhyme in book form with cute illustrations by Steven Kellogg.

Beal, Kathleen. *Here, It's Winter*. Addison Wesley, 1994. 15" × 18", $16.95, Gr 1. One of a set of Big Books made especially for singing along. Uses rhythm, rhyme, and repetition to build language skills. The characters and songs in this set are multicultural. Other titles are *I Like You, I Love My Family*, and *Pink, I Think*.

Bemelmans, Ludwig. *Madeline*. Puffin, 1939. 12" × 17", $17.99, Ps–Gr 3. "In an old house in Paris . . . covered with vines, lived twelve little girls in two straight lines . . ." starts the traditional tale that accounts the escapades of the smallest, Madeline.

The Big Alphabet Book. Dominie Press, 1995. 14" × 18", $25.00, Ps. Each letter of the alphabet is represented by both upper and lower case on one page, and accompanied by one large color, clearly labeled illustration.

Blocksma, Mary. *Rub-a-Dub-Dub, What's in the Tub?* Children's Press, 1988. 15½" × 20", $16.99, Gr 1. A boy and his dog have a wonderful time in the bathtub, but try not to get any water on the floor.

Blonder, Ellen. *Noisy Breakfast*. Scholastic, 1989. 15" × 19", $19.95, Gr K–2. Sentences with sound effects describe mouse and dog's noisy meal.

Bogart, Jo Ellen. *10 for Dinner*. Scholastic, 1989. 15" × 19", $24.95, Gr 1–2. A silly counting book about the strange but wonderful guests at a birthday party.

Bolton, Janet. *My Grandmother's Quilt: A Book and Pocketful of Patchwork Pieces*. Celebration Press, 1995. 14" × 18", $20.00, Gr 1. Tells the history and tradition of quilt making as well as tales about the individual cloth scraps.

Borden, Louise. *Caps, Hats, Socks, and Mittens*. Scholastic, 1989. 14¾" × 17¾", $19.95, Ps. Simple text and illustrations describe the pleasures of the seasons.

Bourgeois, Paulette. *Franklin in the Dark*. Scholastic, 1992. 15" × 19", $24.95, Gr K–2. Franklin is a turtle who is so afraid of the dark he won't even stay in his own shell!

———. *Franklin Is Bossy*. Scholastic, 1994. 15" × 19", $24.95, Gr 2–3. A turtle named Franklin realizes that no one likes a bossy friend.

———. *Little Sarah's Big Boots*. Scholastic, 1989. 15" × 19", $24.95, Gr K–2. Sarah is dismayed to find out she has outgrown her favorite pair of yellow rain boots.

Brett, Jan. *The Mitten*. Scholastic, 1992. 15" × 18", $24.95, Ps–Gr 3. Several animals sleep snugly in Nicki's lost white mitten until the bear sneezes.

Brown, Margaret Wise. *Big Red Barn*. HarperCollins, 1989. 15" × 17¾", $19.95,

Ps. A rhyming story that chronicles the activities of barnyard animals all through a day.

———. *Goodnight Moon*. Scholastic, 1989. 15" × 17½", $19.95, Ps. Goodnight is said by a baby bunny to each of the objects in the Great Green Room.

Brown, Ruth. *A Dark Dark Tale*. Dial Books for Young Readers, 1991. 14" × 17", $17.95, Ps. Journeying through a dark house, a black cat surprises its only inhabitant, a mouse.

Browne, Anthony. *Things I Like*. Houghton Mifflin, 1989. 15" × 19", $27.99, Ps. A chimpanzee talks about the games and toys he likes to play.

Bunting, Eve. *Rabbit's Party*. Scholastic, 1990. 14" × 17", $19.95, Gr K–2. Rabbit wants to have a party in this basic introduction to adding.

Butler, Alyson. *DeColores*. Teaching Resource Center, 1993. 12" × 18", $12.95, Ps. A fourteen page book of both the English and Spanish translations of this popular Spanish song.

———. *Mary Wore Her Red Dress*. Teaching Resource Center, 1993. 12" × 18", $12.95, Ps. A rhyming children's song about colors illustrated with pen and ink. This book is spiral bound.

Butler, Andrea. *Jeb's Barn*. Celebration Press, 1995. 14" × 18", $20.00, Ps. An old fashioned barn raising is illustrated and the days of the week are introduced.

Calmenson, Stephanie. *It Begins With an A*. Morrow/Mulberry, 1994. 16" × 18¾", $19.95, Gr 1. A series of rhyming riddles introduce the letters of the alphabet.

Carle, Eric. *The Grouchy Ladybug*. Scholastic, 1986. 15" × 18", $24.95, Ps. The ladybug is mean to everyone until she meets a whale.

———. *Have You Seen My Cat?* Scholastic, 1991. 15" × 18", $24.95, Gr K–1. A young boy searching for his cat encounters fabulous felines.

———. *A House for Hermit Crab*. Scholastic, 1987. 15" × 18", $19.95, Gr 1–2. A hermit crab that has outgrown his shell moves into a new home, which he decorates to reflect the undersea animals he has met while traveling there.

———. *The Lamb and the Butterfly*. Scholastic, 1996. 15" × 18", $24.95, Ps. A lamb and a butterfly meet and learn all about each other's lives.

———. *Pancakes, Pancakes*. Scholastic, 1991. 15½" × 21½", $19.95, Ps–Gr 1. Jack wants pancakes for breakfast, but his mother is busy. He must do chores such as cut the wheat, make flour, fetch an egg, milk the cow, and so on, all to get his breakfast.

———. *The Tiny Seed*. Simon and Schuster, 1991. 15½" × 21½", $24.95, Ps. The story of the life cycle of a flower from seed to mature flower.

———. *Today Is Monday*. Putnam, 1993. 15" × 18", $24.95, Ps–Gr 1. The names of the days of the week are introduced in a rhyme.

———. *The Very Hungry Caterpillar*. Putnam, 1994. 15" × 18", $24.95, Ps–Gr 1. A caterpillar eats through the pages of the book to metamorphosis.

Carlson, Nancy. *I Like Me!* Puffin, 1991. 13¼" × 17", $17.99, Ps. Louanne is a charming pig who relays the message that one can have fun, admire oneself, and take care, even when all alone.

Carlstrom, Nancy White. *Swim the Silver Sea, Joshie Otter*. Putnam, 1993. 15" × 18", $24.95, Gr 1–2. A bedtime lullaby illustrates the special bond between mother and child.

Carmine, Mary. *Daniel's Dinosaurs*. Scholastic, 1995. 15" × 18", $24.95, Gr 1–2.

Daniel's worried mom takes him to the aquarium to get his mind off dinosaurs.

Carter, David. *Over in the Meadow*. Scholastic, 1992. 14¼" × 18½", 19.95, Ps. Interesting paint applications illustrate this poem that describes the activities of various animals and the numbers 1–10.

Cauley, Lorinda B. *Clap Your Hands*. Putnam, 1992. 15" × 19", $24.95, Ps–K. A wonderful read-aloud rhyme featuring a clap hands and stomp feet rhyme.

Chase, Edith. *The New Baby Calf*. Scholastic, 1991. 15" × 18", $24.95, Gr K–1. Plasticine molded illustrations show the growth of a calf.

Child, Lydia. *Over the River and Through the Wood*. Mulberry, 1989. 14" × 18½", $18.95, Ps. Scenes from a rural New England town illustrate this familiar Thanksgiving song about the holiday at grandmother's house.

Cohen, Caron Lee. *The Mud Pony*. Scholastic, 1995. 14½" × 17½", $24.95, Gr 1–3. A Native American tale about a magical pony made of mud.

Cole, Joanna. *The Magic School Bus at the Waterworks*. Scholastic, 1991. 15" × 18", $21.90, Gr 1–3. Ms. Frizzle takes her class on a field trip to the waterworks, and no one is surprised when they magically learn about water purification from the inside out.

———. *The Magic School Bus Inside the Earth*. Scholastic, 1987. 15" × 18", $21.90, Gr 1–3. Ms. Frizzle's class learns first hand about different kinds of rocks and the formation of the earth.

———. *The Magic School Bus Inside the Human Body*. Scholastic, 1989. 15" × 18", $21.90, Gr 1–3. A special field trip on the magic school bus allows Ms. Frizzle's class to look at the major parts of the body and how they work.

———. *The Magic School Bus Lost in the Solar System*. Scholastic, 1990. 15" × 18", $21.90, Gr 1–3. Ms. Frizzle's class goes to outer space and visits each planet in the solar system.

———. *The Magic School Bus on the Ocean Floor*. Scholastic, 1992. 15" × 18", $21.90, Gr 1–3. On another special field trip on the magic school bus, Ms. Frizzle's class learns about the ocean and the creatures that live there.

———. *This Is the Place for Me*. Permabound, 1990. 15" × 18", $33.99, Ps. A short, touching story about belonging featuring a bear looking for home. Please note that book is hardbound raising the price substantially.

Cowcher, Helen. *Antarctica*. Scholastic, 1990. 15" × 19", $24.95, Gr K–2. Wedell seals, skuas, and the other animals of Antarctica are shown.

———. *Rainforest*. Scholastic, 1991. 15" × 19", $24.95, Gr 3. Exotic animals watch as man and machine threaten to destroy the rainforest.

———. *Whistling Thorns*. Scholastic, 1994. 15" × 19¼", $19.95, Gr 2–up. The relationships of African wildlife are shown in this story about how a plant in nature discourages overgrazing.

Cowen-Fletcher, Jane. *It Takes a Village*. Scholastic, 1994. 17⅛" × 18⅞", $19.95, Gr 1–up. Based on the proverb "It takes a whole village to raise a child," this book explores the people and their relationships in an African village.

———. *Mama Zooms*. Scholastic, 1993. 14½" × 16½", $19.95, Ps. A boy's wonderful mom gets around and takes him zooming in her wheelchair.

Cowley, Joy. *Mrs. Wishy-Washy*. The Wright Group, 1990. 15" × 18", $25.00, Gr 1–2. A cow, a pig, and a duck play in the mud until Mrs. Wishy-Washy comes along to give them a bath.

Crews, Donald. *Freight Train*. Mulberry, 1993. 17⅞" × 14½", $18.95, Ps. Brief text and colorful pictures track the journey of a train as it goes through tunnels, by cities, and over trestles.

———. *School Bus*. Morrow, 1993. 17⅞" × 14½", $24.95, Ps. A simply written, brightly illustrated book about school buses and the children who ride them.

———. *Ten Black Dots*. Scholastic, 1993. 17⅞" × 14½", $24.95, Gr K. Children count their way to ten with simple rhymes and brightly colored objects.

———. *Truck*. Mulberry, 1980. 17" × 13½", $18.95, Ps. Follows the journey of a truck from loading to unloading.

Crowser, J. *Keeping Silkworms*. Hawthorne Press, 1991. 15" × 18", $24.50, Gr 2. A beginning reader all about silkworms illustrated with glossy color photos.

Curran, Eileen. *Easter Parade*. Troll, 1985. 16" × 19", $14.95, Gr 1. With Nancy's help, the Easter Bunny is able to provide presents that make everyone happy, until it is discovered there is nothing left for little Nancy.

Dabcovich, Lydia. *Sleepy Bear*. Puffin, 1993. 17⅞" × 15", $17.99, Ps. Bear gets ready for winter and hibernation and his awakening in the spring.

Dale, Christine. *The Ivy*. Scholastic, 1989. 15" × 19", $24.95, Gr 2–3. A cautionary tale about an ivy plant that outgrows its welcome.

Degen, Bruce. *Jamberry*. HarperCollins, 1983. 15" × 19¼", $19.95, Ps–Gr 1. A little boy walking in the forest meets a big lovable bear that takes him on a delicious berry picking adventure in the magical world of Berryland.

De Paola, Tomie. *Charlie Needs a Cloak*. Simon and Schuster, 1982. 14" × 18", $24.95, Gr 1–2. Charlie is a shepherd who makes a cloak from wool to finish.

———. *The Legend of the Indian Paintbrush*. Putnam, 1991. 14" × 18", $24.95, Gr K–2. A retelling of the Native American legend that explains the origin of the Indian Paintbrush flower.

———. *Strega Nona*. Scholastic, 1992. 14" × 18", $19.95, Gr 1–3. When Strega Nona leaves him in charge of her magic pasta pot, Big Anthony is determined to show the townspeople how it works.

De Vries, John. *In My Backyard*. Collier, 1993. 15" × 19", $19.95, Gr K–2. Rhyme, repetition, and picture cues help kids to read this realistic story about a boy and his pets.

Dodds Dayle Ann. *Wheel Away!* Scholastic, 1991. 14" × 17", $21.90, Gr K–1. A runaway wheel takes a bumpy, bouncy, noisy journey through town.

Donnelly, Liza. *Dinosaur Garden*. Scholastic, 1991. 15" × 19", $24.95, Ps–1. Rex and his dog Bones plant a dinosaur garden and are joined by some huge dinosaur guests.

Dorros, Arthur. *Animal Tracks*. Scholastic, 1991. 18" × 15", $19.95, Gr 1–3. This book introduces signs and tracks left by animals such as a raccoon, duck, frog, black bear, and human.

———. *This Is My House*. Scholastic, 1992. 18" × 15", $24.95, Gr 2–3. Readers learn about materials, sizes, and shapes of houses around the world.

Drew, David. *Animal, Plant, or Mineral*. Thomas Nelson Australia, 1988. 15" × 18", $19.99, Gr 1. Using various creatures, this book introduces inquiry skills such as seeing, inferring, and predicting.

———. *Hidden Animals*. Thomas Nelson Australia, 1988. 15" × 18", $19.99, Gr 1. A picture book format guessing game using animals as catalysts to explain camouflage.

————. *The Life of a Butterfly*. Thomas Nelson, 1987. 15" × 18", $19.99, Gr 1. Explains the life cycle of a butterfly.

————. *Postcards from the Planets*. Thomas Nelson, 1988. 15" × 18", $19.99, Gr 1. This book gives simple information about the solar system.

————. *Tadpole Diary*. Thomas Nelson, 1988. 15" × 18", $19.99, Gr 1. Introduces the life cycle of a frog.

————. *What Is It?* Thomas Nelson, 1987. 15" × 18", $19.99, Gr 1. Inquiry skills such as seeing, inferring, and predicting are introduced through various objects.

Dunbar, Joyce. *Ten Little Mice*. HBJ, 1990. 14½" × 18", $19.95, Gr 1-3. A subtraction counting book featuring ten beautifully illustrated mice who each scurry home.

Dunrea, Olivier. *Noggin and Bobbin in the Garden*. Celebration Press, 1995. 14" × 18", $20.00, Gr 1. A father and child moles tend their lovely garden.

Ehlert, Lois. *Eating the Alphabet: Fruits from A to Z*. HBJ, 1989. 14" × 17⅞", $19.95, Gr 1–3. An alphabetical tour of the world of fruits and vegetables from apricot and artichoke to yam and zucchini.

————. *Feathers for Lunch*. HBJ, 1990. 11½" × 17½", $19.95, Ps. An escaped house cat encounters twelve birds in the backyard, but is unable to catch any of them. As a result, he has feathers to eat.

————. *Growing Vegetable Soup*. HBJ, 1987. 18" × 18", $18.95, Ps–Gr 3. A father and small child grow their own vegetables then make them into soup.

————. *Planting a Rainbow*. HBJ, 1988. 14" × 18", $19.95, Ps–Gr 3. A mother and child plant a variety of flowers that have various colors in the family garden.

Emberley, Rebecca. *Taking a Walk: A Book in Two Languages/Caminadpo: Un Libro Dos Lenguas*. Scholastic, 1992. 18" × 18", $19.95, Gr 1–3. English and Spanish labeled illustrations introduce the things a child might see when taking a walk.

Epstein, Elaine. *Say It, Sign It*. Scholastic, 1995. 15" × 18", $19.95, Gr K–2. Using American Sign Language, Todd and Sonya enjoy a day at the beach.

Evans, Kate. *Hunky Dory Found It*. Houghton Mifflin, 1995. 16" × 17½", $27.93, Ps. Hunky Dory, an adorable but sometimes bad dog, finds a lost object.

Everitt, Lucy. *Mean Soup*. HBJ, 1992. 18" × 18", $19.95, Ps–Gr 3. Horace feel really mean after a bad day until he helps his mother make a pot of mean soup.

Fleming, Denise. *In the Tall, Tall Grass*. Henry Holt, 1993. 18½" × 18½", $19.95, Ps–Gr 3. Rhymed text presents a toddler's view of creatures found in the grass from lunchtime to sundown.

Florian, Douglas. *Vegetable Garden*. HBJ, 1994. 13⅞" × 18", $19.95, Ps. Rhyming text describes how a family plants a vegetable garden and helps it grow to a rich harvest.

Fowler, Allan. *Tasting Things*. Children's Press, 1991. 15" × 18", $19.95, Gr 1–3. A Rookie Read-About Science book featuring multi-ethnic children using all of their senses. Indexed.

Fox, Mem. *Hattie and the Fox*. Bradbury, 1986. 15" × 19", $16.95, Ps. A cumulative tale with repeated phrases for joining in about a hen that warns the other farm animals of an approaching fox.

————. *Night Noises*. Gulliver Books/HBJ, 1991. 14" × 17", $19.95, Ps–Gr 2. Old Lilly Laceby dozes by the fire with her faithful dog, but she is soon awoken by strange noises that bring a big surprise.

Franco, Betsy. *Bo and Peter*. Scholastic, 1993. 14" × 18", $19.95, Gr K–2. The story of best friends and what they like to do together.

Frazier, Debra. *On the Day You Were Born.* Harcourt Brace, 1991. 14" × 18", $19.95, Gr 1–3. The earth celebrates the birth of a newborn baby.

Freeman, Don. *Corduroy.* Scholastic, 1991. 14" × 20", $21.90, Gr 1–3. Well-known story of the adventures of a stuffed bear waiting to be chosen by a child in the toy department of a large store.

———. *A Pocket for Corduroy.* Scholastic, 1991. 14" × 20", $21.90, Gr 1–2. The sequel to *Corduroy* in which the bear is lost in a laundromat.

Gelman, Rita. *Hello, Cat You Need a Hat.* Scholastic, 1993. 15" × 18", $24.95, Gr K–1. A mouse with a huge supply of hats tries to annoy a cat into wearing one.

———. *More Spaghetti, I Say.* Permabound, 1989. 15" × 18", $33.99, Ps. A child extols the virtues of spaghetti over all other foods.

———. *Why Can't I Fly?* Scholastic, 1989. 15" × 18", $28.99, Ps. Minnie the monkey seeks the help of a bird, ladybug, duck, and butterfly to help her learn to fly.

Gibbons, Gail. *Happy Birthday.* Scholastic, 1996. 15" × 18", $24.95, Gr 1–2. Children will find out all about birthday celebrations, flowers, gemstones, and astrological signs.

———. *The Milk Makers.* Simon and Schuster, 1987. 15" × 18", $24.95, Gr 1–3. A look at the different machines and processes milk goes through before being poured into a glass.

Gibson, Akimi. *Don't Be Late.* Scholastic, 1994. 15" × 18", $19.95, Gr K–2. A repetitive and rhyming message is passed from one animal to another.

Giganti, Paul. *Each Orange Had 8 Slices.* Mulberry, 1994. 17⅞" × 14½", $18.95, Gr 1–3. A simple, brightly illustrated introduction to counting and adding.

———. *Notorious Numbers.* Teaching Resource Center, 1993. 12" × 18", $12.95, Gr 2. A teddy bear character asks kids to think about what comes in groups of 1's, 2's, 3's, etc.

Gilman, Phoebe. *Something from Nothing.* Scholastic, 1993. 15" × 18", $24.95, Gr 1–3. Joseph's grandpa makes all kinds of things from old items.

Ginsburg, Mirra. *Across the Stream.* Scholastic, 1989. 15" × 19", $18.90, Ps. The story of a clever hen that uses the swimming talents of her friend the duck to escape a fox. Told in rhyme with many repetitions.

———. *The Chick and the Duckling.* Houghton Mifflin, 1988. 15" × 19", $27.99, Ps. A duckling makes friends with a baby chick, who tries to do everything the duck does.

Glazer, Tom. *On Top of Spaghetti.* Celebration Press, 1995. 14" × 18", $20.00, Gr 1. The favorite children's song illustrated.

Goldish, Meisha. *Paper Party.* Newbridge, 1992. 14½" × 19½", $14.90, Ps. This book has a rhymed text with a minimum amount of words and shows many simple items that are created by young children using different types of paper. Not a primary purchase.

Gomi, Taro. *My Friends.* Scholastic, 1996. 15" × 19", $24.95, Ps. Vibrant illustrations and simple text are blended together as a girl recounts all she has learned from her friends.

Gordon, Gaelyn. *Duckat.* Scholastic, 1993. 15" × 19", $24.95, Ps–2. A little girl befriends a very unusual duck—one who thinks he's a cat!

Graham, A. *Cinderella/Alex and the Glass Slipper.* Hawthorne, 1992. 14" × 18", $29.00, Gr 3. Cinderella story with a twist.

Graves, Kimberlee. *I Can't Sleep.* Creative Teaching Press, 1994. 12" x 18", $7.95, Gr 2. Controlled vocabulary reader introduces the concept of matter. Eight pages; not a primary purchase.

———. *Is It Alive?* Creative Teaching Press, 1994. 12" × 18", $7.95, Gr 1. This very easy reader is eight pages long and shows what is alive and not alive. Not a primary purchase.

———. *My Mom Can Fix Anything.* Creative Teaching Press, 1994. 12" × 18", $7.95, Gr 2. A child's mother fixes everything that is broken with her tools in this eight-page reader. Not a primary purchase.

———. *See How It Grows.* Creative Teaching Press, 1994. 12" × 18", $7.95, Gr 1. Life cycles of animals and plants are shown in this eight-page reader. Not a primary purchase.

Graves, Kimberlee and Rozanne Williams. *Where Are You Going?* Creative Teaching Press, 1994. 12" × 18", $7.95, Gr 2. The five senses and their sensations are explored through a trip around the neighborhood. Not a primary purchase.

Grbich, Aaron. *Three Little Kittens.* Teaching Resource Center, 1990. 12" × 18", $12.95, Ps. The traditional rhyme about three careless baby cats is told in a contemporary setting. Not a primary purchase.

Greydanus, Rose. *The Valentine's Day Grump.* Troll, 1981. 16" × 19", $14.95, Gr 1. A Valentine might make Gus the Grump happy, but everyone is afraid to give him one.

Grossman, Bill. *Tommy at the Grocery Store.* HarperCollins, 1989. 15" × 19", $19.95, Gr 1–3. Tommy is a small pig whose mother accidentally leaves him at the grocery store. After that he is bought several times by silly adult pigs who mistake him for a sausage, potato, bottle, corn, a banana, a chair, a table, etc.

Grossman, Patricia. *The Night Ones.* HBJ, 1991. 15" × 19", $24.95, Gr K–2. A glimpse of the mysterious nighttime world that comes to life when most people are asleep.

Hajdusiewicz, Babs Bell. *Jacks and More Jacks.* Celebration Press, 1995. 15" × 18", $20.00, Gr 1. All about the different "Jacks" found in nursery rhymes and stories, such as "Jack Be Nimble" and "Jack and the Beanstalk."

Hale, Sarah. *Mary Had a Little Lamb.* Scholastic, 1990. 15" × 18", $24.95, Ps. A color photographed contemporary rendition of the traditional rhyme.

Hall, Donald. *The Ox-Cart Man.* Puffin, 1983. 14½" × 17½", $24.95, Gr 1–2. A Caldecott award winning book about a nineteenth-century traveling salesman.

Hammond, Franklin. *Ten Little Ducks.* Firefly, 1992. 16" × 16", $24.95, Ps. Readers count ten little ducks doing their favorite activities.

Hamsa, Bobbie. *Fast Draw Freddie.* Children's Press, 1984. 15½" × 20", $13.44, Gr 1. Fast draw Freddie draws all kinds of pictures fast: big, small, fat, cat, and pictures of Mom and Dad, too.

Hardin, Suzanne. *What Do You Do?* Celebration Press, 1995. 14" × 18", $20.00, Gr 1. A rhyming animals counting book with controlled vocabulary.

Hayes, Sarah. *This Is the Bear.* Candlewick, 1992. 14⅞" × 18", $19.95, Ps. A toy bear is accidentally taken to the dump but is rescued by a dog.

———. *This Is the Bear and the Picnic Lunch.* Candlewick, 1993. 14⅞" × 18", $27.93, Ps. A toy bear has a small adventure while on a picnic with his boy owner.

Hazen, Barbara. *Let's Go!* Newbridge, 1992. 14½" × 19¾", $14.90, Ps. Two children journey across town to grandmother's in this rhymed text.

———. *Pass the Cheese, Please.* Newbridge, 1992. 14½" × 19¾", $14.90, Ps. Cute cartoon mice explain manners in this minimum text rhyme.

———. *Who Lost a Shoe?* Newbridge, 1992. 14½" × 19¾", $14.90, Ps. Rhymed verse featuring an owl determined to find the owner of a lost red shoe.

Heller, Ruth. *A Cache of Jewels and Other Collective Nouns.* Putnam, 1989. 14" × 19", $24.95, Gr 3. A "gam" of whales, a "parcel" of penguins, and other collective nouns.

———. *Chickens Aren't the Only Ones.* Scholastic, 1981. 14" × 19", $19.95, Gr 1–3. A popular nonfiction rhyming tale about animals that lay eggs.

———. *Kites Sail High.* Scholastic, 1991. 14" × 19", $21.90, Gr 1–3. An exploration of verbs featuring bright, bold illustrations and snappy rhythmic text.

———. *Many Luscious Lollipops: A Book About Adjectives.* Putnam, 1992. 14" × 19", $24.95, Gr 3. With simple verse and bright paintings, this book explains adjectives.

———. *Merry Go Round: A Book About Nouns.* Putnam, 1990. 14" × 19", $24.95, Gr 3. Funny, rhyming text defines concrete, abstract, possessive, and plural nouns.

———. *The Reason for a Flower.* Putnam, 1983. 14" × 19", $21.90, Gr 1–3. Various concepts in relation to the broad topic of plants are introduced. Includes some harder vocabulary.

———. *Up, Up, and Away: A Book About Adverbs.* Putnam, 1991. 14" × 19", $24.95, Gr 3. A story about superlatives, double negatives, and irregular verbs.

Hennessy, B.G. *Jake Baked the Cake.* Scholastic, 1992. 23" × 23", $19.95, Ps. Rhymed verse about a wedding with the phrase "Jake baked the cake." repeated often. Very large book!

———. *School Days.* Viking, 1990. 18" × 20", $24.95, Gr K–1. Follow the day of a high-spirited group of classmates.

Hill, S. *Poems Not to Be Missed.* Hawthorne, 1990. 15" × 18", $29.00, Gr 3. Collection of poetry with subjects that are dear and familiar to children.

Hirschi, Ron. *Spring.* Dutton, 1990. 14½" × 17⅞", $24.95, Gr 1–2. The winter snow is gone and spring is here. This book is illustrated will full color photos.

Hoban, Russell. *Bread and Jam for Frances.* Harper Trophy, 1993. 15" × 19", $19.95, Ps. A new, four-color edition of this classic tale about picky eaters.

Hoban, Tana. *26 Letters and 99 Cents.* Greenwillow, 1988. 15" × 19", $24.95, Ps. A dual-purpose tool that uses photos of plastic letters and numbers to teach.

———. *Look! Look! Look!* Greenwillow, 1989. 15" × 19", $24.95, Ps. Unusual photographs teach young readers different ways to look at familiar objects.

———. *Of Colors and Things.* Greenwillow, 1988. 15" × 19", $24.95, Ps. Photo groups of familiar items demonstrate color, shape, and other concepts.

Hobermann, Mary Ann. *A House Is a House for Me.* Scholastic, 1984. 15" × 19", $19.95, Ps–Gr 3. This book lists in rhyme the various dwelling places of animals, people, and other objects.

Hoffman, Beverly. *Diana Made Dinner.* Dominie Press, 1995. 14" × 19", $15.00, Gr 2. An eighty-one word count controlled-vocabulary story about cooking.

———. *My Dad Cooks.* Dominie Press, 1995. 14" × 19", $15.00, Gr 1. A twenty-nine word count controlled-vocabulary book about a father who likes to cook.

Howard, Elizabeth. *Aunt Flossie's Hats (and Crab Cakes Later).* Scholastic, 1996. 14" × 16", $24.95, Ps. Two little girls visit

Aunt Flossie, try on her hats, and listen to stories about each hat.

Hutchins, Pat. *Don't Forget the Bacon*. Mulberry, 1994. 17⅞" × 14½", $18.95, Ps. A young boy walks to the grocery store for his mother and tries to remember everything he is supposed to buy. Along the way, his list becomes garbled when he talks to those he meets.

————. *The Doorbell Rang*. Mulberry, 1994. 17⅞" × 14½", $18.95, Ps. Each time the doorbell rang, more friends arrived to share in a batch of Ma's yummy cookies.

————. *Good Night Owl!* Aladdin, 1991. 15" × 18", $16.95, Ps. Owl tries to go to sleep during the day, but he is bothered by the sounds of one animal after another.

————. *Rosie's Walk*. Scholastic, 1987. 15" × 18", $19.95, Ps. A wily fox follows and tries to catch Rosie as she casually saunters all around the barnyard in this almost wordless story.

————. *The Surprise Party!* Aladdin, 1991. 14" × 18", $16.95, Ps. Rabbit lets it slip that there is a surprise party for owl, but in the classic form of gossip, owl misunderstands and the message is garbled as it passes through the lips of each animal.

————. *The Wind Blew*. Scholastic, 1996. 14" × 18", $24.95, Gr K-1. The wind snatches away pedestrian's possessions.

James, Simon. *Dear Mr. Blueberry*. Celebration Press, 1995. 14" × 18", $20.00, Ps. A young girl and her teacher correspond about the whale she has discovered in her pond.

Johnston, Tony. *The Quilt Story*. Putnam, 1990. 15" × 18", $24.94, Gr 2–3. A beautiful quilt links two little girls across the generations in this story of comfort.

Joose, Barbara M. *Mama, Do You Love Me?* Scholastic, 1992. 16" × 16", $19.95, Ps. A child living in the Arctic learns the unconditional nature of mother's love.

Kalan, Robert. *Jump, Frog, Jump!* Scholastic, 1994. 15" × 20", $19.95, Ps. A cumulative tale in which a frog tries to catch a fly while avoiding capture himself.

Kasza, Keiko. *A Mother for Choco*. Houghton Mifflin, 1992. 14" × 18", $27.99, Ps. A young bird learns that families don't have to look the same to be full of love.

Keats, Ezra Jack. *Peter's Chair*. HarperCollins, 1992. 15" × 19", $19.95, Ps–Gr 1. When Peter discovers that all his old baby furniture is being painted pink for the arrival of his new baby sister, he rescues a blue chair and then runs away.

————. *The Snowy Day*. Puffin, 1978. 15" × 19", $19.95, Ps. Shows the adventures of a city boy on a very snowy day.

Kellogg, Steven. *The Mysterious Tadpole*. A Puffin Pied Piper Giant, 1992. 14½" × 19", $17.99, Gr 1–3. It soon becomes clear that Louie's pet tadpole is not turning into an ordinary frog.

————. *Paul Bunyan*. Mulberry, 1984. 13¼" × 17½", $18.95, Gr 1–3. The tale of the giant Paul and his blue ox Babe told with style, exaggeration, and wonderful pictures by Kellogg.

————. *Pinkerton, Behave!* Dial Books for Young Readers, 1979. 14½" × 18", $16.95, Gr 1–3. Although Pinkerton the great dane's behavior is unconventional, in the end it makes no difference to his becoming a hero.

Kelly, Patricia. *Mr. Cricket Finds a Friend*. Dominie Press, 1985. 14" × 19", $20.00, Gr 3. A 139 count controlled-vocabulary story about a lonely cricket that finds a friend by playing a song.

Kitamura, Satoshi. *From Acorn to Zoo*. Scholastic, 1996. 14½" × 19", $24.95, Gr 1–2. A delightfully illustrated alphabet book brings silliness to learning the alphabet.

————. *UFO Diary*. Farrar, 1991. 14½" × 19", $24.95, Ps–K. A little boy and a space visitor explore the earth and heavens.

Kowalczyk, Carolyn. *Purple Is Part of a Rainbow*. Children's Press, 1985. 15½" × 20", $19.99, Gr 2. Introduces vocabulary and the concept of parts of a whole with examples such as a petal on a flower and a whisker on a kitty.

Kraus, Robert. *Whose Mouse Are You?* Scholastic, 1991. 15" × 18", $19.95, Ps. A lonely little mouse must be resourceful in order to bring his mouse family back together.

Langstaff, John. *Over in the Meadow*. HBJ, 1957. 14" × 20", $19.95, Ps. A traditional rhyme that introduces animals and their youngsters using numbers.

Lee, Dennis. *The Dennis Lee Big Book of Poetry*. Dominie Press, 1995. 15" × 18", Gr 1 and up. A spiral-bound collection of humorous poetry by a noted children's author.

Leedy, Loreen. *The Bunny Play*. Scholastic, 1996. 15" × 18", $24.95, Gr 2–3. The bunnies decide to put on a musical stage version of *Little Red Riding Hood*.

————. *The Furry News: How to Make a Newspaper*. Henry Holt, 1990. 15" × 18", $24.95, Gr 1–2. A group of animals show how to make a neighborhood newspaper.

Lille, Patricia. *When This Box Is Full*. Greenwillow, 1993. 14½" × 17⅞", $24.95, Gr 1–2. Children learn about the seasons in this wonderfully illustrated book in which a child adds memorable objects to a special box.

Lillegard, Dee. *Frog's Lunch*. Scholastic, 1996. 15" × 18", $19.95, Gr K–2. Frog is sitting on a lily pad and along comes an unsuspecting fly right at lunchtime.

————. *Sitting In My Box*. Puffin Unicorn, 1989. 16" × 20", $17.99, Ps. A boy takes his book inside a large discarded carton, and soon animals from his story join him and disrupt his solitude.

Lindbergh, Reeve. *The Day the Goose Got Loose*. Scholastic, 1996. 16" × 20", $24.95, Gr 1–2. Children will laugh as this frisky goose runs around the farm freeing the other animals.

Ling, Bettina. *Kites*. Scholastic, 1996. 15" × 18", $19.95, Gr K–2. Kites of different sizes, shapes, and colors splash in the sky.

Lionni, Leo. *A Busy Year*. Knopf, 1992. 15" × 18", $24.95, Gr K–2. Two mice take care of a special tree throughout the seasons.

————. *A Color of His Own*. Knopf, 1993. 15" × 18", $24.95, Ps–1. Chameleon tries very hard to stay one color, but cannot. He is not happy until he finds a new friend.

————. *Swimmy*. Scholastic, 1996. 15" × 18", $24.95, Gr K–2. A little fish and his friend triumph over a big fish.

Livingston, Myra Cohn. *Space Songs*. Henry Holt, 1988. 12" × 18", $24.95, Gr K–3. A collection of poems and bold illustrations about outer space.

Lobel, Arnold. *On Market Street*. Permabound, 1981. 15" × 18", $33.67, Ps. A child buys presents from A to Z as he shops along Market Street.

Lunn, Carolyn. *Bobby's Zoo*. Children's Press, 1989. 15½" × 20", $19.99, Gr 2. Bobby doesn't know what to do with all the animals that are in his house.

————. *A Whisper Is Quiet*. Children's Press, 1988. 15½" × 20", $19.99, Gr 1. Presents pairs of things with contrasting qualities, such as the hot sun and cold ice cream, or a quiet whisper and a loud band.

McCloskey, Robert. *Make Way for Ducklings*. Puffin, 1991. 16" × 20", $17.95, Ps–Gr 3. Mr. and Mrs. Mallard are very proud of their duckling children as they walk to their home in the Boston Public Garden.

McDaniel, Becky. *Katie Did It*. Children's Press, 1983. 15¼" × 20", $19.95, Gr 1. Katie, the youngest of three children, always gets the blame for everything bad until she does something good for a change.

McDermott, Gerald. *Zomo the Rabbit*. HBJ, 1992. 16¾" × 20", $24.95, Gr 2–3. Zomo the Rabbit is not big or strong, but he is very clever! He makes a deal with the sky god to earn wisdom.

McKissack, Patricia, and Fredrick McKissack. *Bugs!* Children's Press, 1988. 15¼" × 20", $19.95, Gr 1. Simple controlled vocabulary and illustrations introduce a variety of insects and the numbers 1–5.

———. *Who Is Coming?* Children's Press, 1988. 15½" × 20", $19.99, Gr 1. A little African monkey runs away from all the dangerous animals except one.

McLean, Anne. *The Bus Ride Big Book*. Dominie Press, 1995. 15" × 18", $50.00, Gr 1. Various animals ride the bus with humorous results. Price reflects hard binding on book.

McMillan, Bruce. *Eating Fractions*. Scholastic, 1991. 18¼" × 15", $19.95, Gr 1. The concept of whole, half, one-third, and one-fourth are pictured in this partially bilingual book about food. Recipes for foods shown are included in the back of the book.

———. *Going on a Whale Watch*. Scholastic, 1992. 14¾" × 16½", $19.95, Gr 1–3. Color photos taken in the Gulf of Maine show the life, anatomy, and eating habits of whales.

———. *Time To . . .* Putnam, 1990. 14¾" × 16½", $24.95, Gr K–1. Enjoy a fun-filled day of photographs of a kindergartner as he learns to tell time.

McPhail, David. *Fix-It*. Puffin Unicorn, 1984. 16¾" × 17¼", $17.99, Ps. The repairman tries to fix the TV while Emma's parents try to entertain her. Soon, Emma becomes more interested in reading a book than anything else.

Mackenzie, Leigh. *A Bath for Patches*. Dominie Press, 1995. 14" × 19", $15.00, Gr 2. An eighty-six-word controlled-vocabulary story featuring a young girl attempting to bathe her cat.

Mallet, J., and T. Erin. *Elevator*. Permabound, 1986. 15" × 18", $22.00, Gr 1. Factual information about the workings of a busy apartment elevator.

Maris, Ron. *I Wish I Could Fly*. Scholastic, 1989. 14½" × 17¾", $24.95, Ps. A silly turtle wishes to fly like a bird, but eventually realizes it is okay to be just a turtle.

Marshall, James. *Red Riding Hood*. Puffin, 1993. 15" × 17", $17.99, Ps–Gr 3. The traditional tale of *Little Red Riding Hood* is spiced up with humorous illustrations.

Martin, Bill. *The Happy Hippopotami*. HBJ, 1991. 14" × 18", $19.95, Ps. The hippopotami enjoy a fun holiday on the beach where they wear pajamas, dance the maypole, and play with water guns.

Martin, Bill, and John Archambault. *Knots on a Counting Rope*. Henry Holt, 1993. 17⅞" × 14½", $19.95, Gr 1–3. A grandfather and his blind grandson reminisce about the boy's birth and other special times gone by.

Martin, Bill, Peggy Brogan, and John Archambault. *Sounds Around the Mountain*. DLM, 1990. 14½" × 18", $23.50, Gr 1–3. An anthology of songs and poetry, both familiar and original.

Martin, Bill and Eric Carle. *Polar Bear, Polar Bear, What Do You Hear?* Henry Holt, 1991. 14½" × 18", $18.95, Ps. Zoo animals from a polar bear to a walrus make their characteristic animal sounds, then children imitate them for the zookeeper.

Martin, Mary Jane. *What's Inside?* Scholastic, 1996. 15" × 18", $19.95, Gr K. A clever book that shows various animals that lay eggs and their babies emerging.

Martinez, Alejandro Cruz, and Fernando Olivera. *The Woman Who Outshone the Sun.* Children's Book Press, 1991. 14" × 18", $24.95, Gr 1–2. The story of townspeople who learn to befriend everyone.

Marzollo, Jean. *Happy Birthday, Martin Luther King.* Scholastic, 1993. 15⅛" × 19¼", $19.95, Gr 1–3. A picture book introduction to the life of Martin Luther King, Jr. illustrated with intricate scratchboard pictures by Brian Pinkney.

———. *In 1492.* Scholastic, 1994. 15⅛" × 19¼" $24.95, Gr 2–3. Simple, rhyming couplets tell of Columbus's voyage to the new world.

Matthews, Louise. *Bunches and Bunches of Bunnies.* Scholastic, 1993. 15" × 18", $28.67, Gr 1–3. Busy bunnies demonstrate multiplication using the numbers 1–12.

Matthias, Catherine. *I Love Cats.* Children's Press, 1988. 15½" × 20", $19.99, Gr 1. Other animals may be very nice, but cats are the best ones to love.

Mayer, Mercer. *There's a Nightmare in My Closet.* Dial Books for Young Readers, 1968. 14½" × 18", $16.98, Ps. A small boy relates how he overcame a monster nightmare who lived in his closet but now shares his bed.

———. *What Do You Do With a Kangaroo?* Scholastic, 1973. 17½" × 21½", $19.95, Ps–Gr 2. Various animals invade the rooms in the house of a little girl and disrupt her daily routine.

Medearis, Angela S. *Dancing with the Indians.* Henry Holt, 1991. 15" × 18", $24.95, Gr 2–3. A girl and her family attend the powwow of the Seminole tribe that befriended her grandfather.

———. *Harry's House.* Scholastic, 1996. 15" × 18", $19.95, Gr K–2. A girl and her

mother saw, hammer, and paint to build Harry a new dog house.

———. *Picking Peas for a Penny.* Scholastic, 1993. 15" × 18", $24.95, Gr 1–3. The author's family remembers life on their grandparent's farm during the Depression.

Millios, Rita. *I Am.* Children's Press, 1987. 15½" × 20", $13.44, Gr 1. Contrasts such differences as "I am big, You are small, I am short, You are tall."

———. *Sneaky Pete.* Children's Press, 1989. 15½" × 20", $13.44, Gr 2. Sneaky Pete proves why he is the champion of Hide and Seek.

Mora, Pat. *Agua, Agua, Agua.* Celebration Press, 1995. 14" × 18", $20.00, Gr 1. An English/Spanish edition of Aesop's fable about crow.

Morris, Ann. *Bread, Bread, Bread.* Mulberry, 1993. 17⅛" × 14½", $18.95, Ps. Celebrates many different kinds of bread and how it is eaten all over the world.

———. *Hats, Hats, Hats.* Mulberry, 1993. 17⅞" × 14½", $18.95. Ps. Color photographs illustrate this introduction to head coverings found around the world.

———. *Loving.* Scholastic, 1995. 17⅞" × 14½", $24.95, Ps. Love is a universal language as the reader learns in this richly photographed book of families around the world.

———. *On the Go.* Scholastic, 1994. 17⅞" × 14½", $24.95, Ps. People around the world travel from one place to another in many ways.

Moses, Amy. *I Am an Explorer.* Children's Press, 1990. 15½" × 20", $19.99, Gr 1. During a trip to the park, a child explores an imaginary cave, mountain, jungle, and desert.

Most, Bernard. *The Cow that Went Oink.* HBJ, 1991. 14½" × 18", $19.95, Ps. A cow that oinks and a pig that moos are ridiculed by the other farm animals until they teach each other new sounds.

———. *If the Dinosaurs Came Back*. Harcourt Brace, 1978. 14¼" × 18", $18.95, Gr 1–3. Shows practical and imaginative uses for dinosaurs, such as buses and bridges, if they came back in modern times.

———. *Zoodles*. HBJ, 1994. 18" × 13⅞", $19.95, Gr 3. A collection of riddles about fanciful animals such as the "kangarooster" (a kangaroo who wakes you up in the morning).

Munsch, Robert. *Love You Forever*. Firefly, 1986. 15½" × 15½", $19.95, Gr 1–3. The tender story of a mother's love for her son that reaches across the generations.

Murphy, Jill. *What Next, Baby Bear!* Dial, 1983. 14½" × 18", $17.99, Ps. While his mother prepares him a bath, Baby Bear makes a quick trip to the moon.

Murphy, Joelle. *Quick, Go Peek!* Celebration Press, 1995. 14" × 18", $20.00, Gr 2. This clever book provides answers to questions such as "What happens when I close the refrigerator door?"

Myers, Bernice. *Because of a Sneeze*. Macmillan, 1992. 14½" × 19¾", $14.90, Ps. A cumulative tale that begins with a sneeze and ends with the pigs loose on the farm.

Neasi, Barbara. *Just Like Me*. Children's Press, 1984. 15½" × 20", $19.99, Gr 1. A little girl describes all of the things she and her twin sister have in common.

———. *Listen to Me*. Children's Press, 1986. 15½" × 20", $19.99, Gr 1. Whenever Mom and Dad are too busy to talk and listen, Grandma saves the day, helping out and being a good listener.

———. *Sweet Dreams*. Children's Press, 1987. 15½" × 20", $19.99, Gr 2. A child describes, in rhyming text and illustrations, all the different kinds of dreams that one can have.

Neitzel, Shirley. *The Jacket I Wear in the Snow*. Scholastic, 1989. 15" × 19", $19.95, Ps. A young girl tells the cumulative tale in rebus of all the clothing she must wear during winter when playing outdoor in the snow.

Noble, Trinka Henkes. *The Day Jimmy's Boa Ate the Wash*. Dial Books for Young Readers, 1991. 14¾" × 18", $17.95, Gr 1–3. Jimmy's pet boa constrictor wreaks havoc during a class trip to the farm.

Numeroff, Laura. *If You Give a Moose a Muffin*. HarperCollins, 1994. 15" × 17", $19.95, Ps. If you give a moose a muffin, chaos will ensue with a string of endless requests.

———. *If You Give a Mouse a Cookie*. Scholastic, 1989. 15" × 17", $18.90, Ps. Mouse will ask for many things once he receives a requested cookie from his human friend.

Oppenheim, Joanne. *Have You Seen Birds?* Permabound, 1993. 15" × 18", $27.00, Gr 1. Rhyming text introduces different varieties of birds and their characteristics. Plasticine molded illustrations.

Parker, John. *I Love Spiders*. Scholastic, 1989. 15" × 18", $24.95, Gr K–1. An interesting twist to people's natural aversion to spiders with a surprise ending.

Parkes, Brenda, and Judith Smith. *The Enormous Watermelon*. Rigby, 1986. 15" × 19", $25.00, Ps. A unique story that includes little picture clues to encourage predictions about what is on the next page. Mother Goose rhyme characters help harvest and eat a watermelon.

Pasternac, Susana. *In the City*. Scholastic, 1996. 15" × 18", $19.95, Gr K–2. This book looks at places in the city, narrowing its focus to one place—a bird's nest.

Pelegrini, Nina. *Families Are Different*. Henry Holt, 1991. 12" × 15", $24.95, Gr 1–2. A sensitive exploration of various types of families.

Peters, Lisa W. *The Sun, the Wind, and the Rain*. Henry Holt, 1991. 12" × 18", $24.95, Gr K–2. By moving back and forth between stories, this book cleverly explains the formation of a mountain by comparing it to a girl's sand creation.

Petrie, Catherine. *Hot Rod Harry*. Children's Press, 1982. 15½" × 20", $19.99, Gr 1. Hot Rod Harry rides so fast on his bike he almost seems to fly like a bird in the air.

Polette, Nancy. *The Little Old Woman and the Hungry Cat*. Morrow/Mulberry, 1994. 14" × 17¾", $18.95, Ps. A very hungry cat eats everyone he sees until he swallows the little old woman who owns him, and she puts an end to his gluttony.

Preller, James. *Wake Me in Spring*. Scholastic, 1996. 15" × 18", $19.95, Gr K–2. Using repetitive sentence patterns, mouse tells bear all he will miss if he hibernates.

Prelutsky, Jack. *Tyrannosaurus Was a Beast*. Mulberry, 1989. 14" × 20", $18.99, Gr 1–3. A collection of humorous poems about dinosaurs.

Racanelli, V. M. *Crunchy, Munchy Cookies*. Newbridge, 1992 14½" × 19¾", $14.99, Ps. The steps and ingredients for making cookies are outlined in rhyme with colorful pictures.

Readhead, Janet S. *The Big Bar of Chocolate*. Scholastic, 1994. 15" × 18", $24.95, Gr K–1. A repetitive tale with a lesson in sharing.

Rees, Mary. *Ten in a Bed*. Houghton Mifflin, 1993. 14½" × 17⅞", $27.99, Ps. An illustrated version of the traditional counting song.

Rey, H.A. *Curious George*. Houghton Mifflin, 1973. 15" x 19", $19.95, Ps. The classic tale of George, a very curious monkey, and his adventures with the man in the yellow hat.

Richards, Nancy W. *Farmer Joe's Hot Day*. Scholastic, 1995. 15" × 18", $24.95, Gr K–1. The story of a hard-working farmer and the strange advice his wife gives him.

Ringgold, Faith. *Tar Beach*. Scholastic, 1994. 15" × 19½", $19.95, Gr 1–3. Cassie lives in an apartment house in Harlem. She takes fantastic imaginary journeys that begin on the "tar beach," the roof of the building.

Robinson, Fay. *We Love Fruit!* Children's Press/Rookie Read About Science, 1993. 16" × 19", $19.95, Gr 1–2. An informational discussion of fruit with a glossary and specific vocabulary.

Rogers, Paul. *What Will the Weather Be Like Today?* Greenwillow, 1990. 15" × 18", $24.95, Gr 1–2. This simple book explores the climates ideal for particular animals all over the world.

Romay, Sarurnino. *Birds on Stage*. Scholastic, 1994. 15" × 18", $19.95, Gr K–2. Read the rhyming riddles and guess which bird will take the spotlight on that page.

Ryder, Joanne. *The Snail's Spell*. Viking, 1992. 15" × 19", $24.95, Gr K–2. This book shows you a garden from the point of view of a snail.

Saksie, Judy. *The Seed Song*. Creative Teaching Press, 1994. 12" × 18", $7.95, Gr 1. A song about planting and growing seeds is illustrated with cut paper collage. Music is included. Eight pages. Not a primary purchase.

Schreiber, Anne. *Log Hotel*. Scholastic, 1994. 15" × 18", $19.95, Gr K–2. In this nonfiction book a tree becomes a log. Animals and plants then move in and cause decay and finally new growth.

Schwartz, David. *How Much Is a Million?* Morrow, 1994. 15" × 18", $19.95, Gr 2–3. Text and pictures try to make possible the conceptualization of a million, a billion, and a trillion.

Seeger, Pete. *Abiyoyo*. Simon and Schuster, 1994. 15" × 18", $24.95, Gr 2–3. A boy and his father are at first rejected by the people of the town, but then use their talents to vanquish Abiyoyo, a terrible giant.

Sendak, Maurice. *Chicken Soup with Rice*. Scholastic, 1986. 14" × 20", $19.95, Ps–Gr 3. This rhymed story uses chicken soup as a unifying theme to present an illustrated tour of all the months of the year.

Serfozo, Mary. *Who Said Red?* Aladdin, 1988. 16" × 18", $18.95, Ps–Gr 1. A dialogue between two children, one of whom prefers red, introduces that color as well as yellow, blue, green, and others.

———. *Who Wants One?* Aladdin, 1989. 16" × 18", $18.95, Ps. Rhyming text and pictures introduce the numbers 1–10.

Sharp, Paul. *Paul the Pitcher*. Children's Press, 1984. 15½" × 20", $19.99, Gr 1. Rhymed text describes the different things that Paul enjoys when he throws a ball.

Shaw, Charles G. *It Looked Like Spilt Milk*. HarperCollins, 1947. 15" × 19", $19.95, Ps. When using your imagination, a cloud can look like many things, from spilled milk, to a flower, to an angel.

Shaw, Nancy. *Sheep in a Jeep*. Houghton Mifflin, 1986. 14" × 18", $27.99, Ps. This rhymed story tells what happens when sheep try to drive.

Sheppard, Jeff. *The Right Number of Elephants*. HarperCollins, 1993. 17" × 14⅞", $19.95, Ps. A counting book explains the right number of elephants needed for various childhood activities.

Shine, Deborah. *Where's the Puppy?* Macmillan, 1992. 14" × 20", $14.90, Ps. Puppy has no place to call his own until Grandpa donates an old rug.

Shulevitz, Uri. *One Monday Morning*. Scholastic, 1974. 15" × 18", $19.95, Ps. A string of imaginary visitors come to see a child who is not at home. Finally, all the guests, including kings and queens, come to visit on a Sunday.

Slobodkina, Esephyr. *Caps for Sale*. Perma-bound, 1985. 15" × 18", $25.99, Ps–Gr 1. A band of tricky monkeys steal the caps from a peddler as he is sleeping under a tree.

Snow, Pegeen. *Eat Your Peas, Louise!* Children's Press, 1985. 15½" × 20", $19.99, Gr 1. Louise is given all sorts of reasons for eating her peas.

Steptoe, John. *Maufaro's Beautiful Daughters*. Lothrop, 1987. 14" × 19", $18.95, Gr 1–3. Mufaro's two beautiful daughters, one bad tempered and one kind and sweet, go before the king who is seeking a wife.

Stevens, Janet. *Three Billy Goats Gruff*. Harcourt Brace, 1987. 15" × 18", $19.95, Ps. Three clever billy goats outwit a big, ugly troll that lives under a bridge they must cross on their way up the mountain.

Tafuri, Nancy. *Have you Seen My Duckling?* Morrow, 1991. 16" × 20", $24.95, Ps. A mother duck searches for her lost duckling.

———. *Spots, Feathers, and Curly Tails*. Houghton Mifflin, 1988. 16" × 20", $27.93, Ps. Farm animals are depicted in bright, big pictures.

Tanner, Jane. *Nicky's Walk*. Modern Curriculum Press, 1989. 16" × 20", $27.99, Ps. On a walk with Mommy, Nicky identifies the colors and objects he sees.

Tello, John. *Amalia and the Grasshopper*. Scholastic, 1995. 15" × 18", $19.95, Gr K–2. Amalia's grandfather and a grasshopper help her solve a basketball problem.

The Three Billy Goats Gruff: A Norwegian Folk Tale. Scholastic, 1984. 15" × 20", $25.99, Ps. Traditional tale of three clever goats who outwit an ugly troll who lives under the bridge they must cross on their way up the mountain.

Titherington, Jeannie. *Pumpkin, Pumpkin*. Scholastic, 1994. 16" × 20", $18.95, Ps. Jamie plants a pumpkin seed and, after watching it grow, carves it and saves some seeds to plant in the spring.

Torres, Esther. *Mi Compleanos*. Teaching Resource Center, 1993. 15" × 18", $12.95, Gr 1. A Spanish language book following the events of a young girl's birthday in Mexico.

Tuchman, Gail. *Swing, Swing, Swing*. Scholastic, 1994. 15" × 18", $19.95, Gr K–2. A frog, a cat, a dog, and a horse join a girl on a swing until she decides to swing alone.

Van Klampen, Vasta. *Orchestranimals*. Scholastic, 1989. 14½" × 17¾", $19.95, Gr 1–3. Various musical instruments found in an orchestra are introduced with unusual animal musicians.

Vaughn, Marcia. *The Old Oak Tree*. Celebration Press, 1995. 14" × 18", $20.00, Gr 1. Black and white illustrations show who lives in the old oak tree. The refrain "But it didn't bother me" is repeated.

Waddell, Martin. *Can't You Sleep, Little Bear?* Candlewick, 1992. 14¾" × 17½", $19.95, Ps. When bedtime comes, Little Bear is afraid of the dark until Big Bear brings him lights and love.

Wallner, John. *City Mouse, Country Mouse*. Scholastic, 1992. 15" × 18¾", $19.95, Ps. Three Aesop's Fables that feature mice are illustrated here: *City Mouse, Country Mouse*; *The Lion and the Mouse*; and *Belling the Cat*.

Walsh, Ellen Stoll. *Mouse Paint*. HBJ, 1991. 14¾" × 18", $19.95, Ps. Three white mice discover jars of red, yellow, and blue paint and then explore the world of color mixing.

Ward, Cindy. *Cookie's Week*. Putnam, 1992. 12" × 18", $24.95, PS. Simple sentences take readers through the days of the week with Cookie, a kitten.

Ward, Lynn. *I Am Eyes—Ni Macho*. Permabound, 1978. 15" × 18", $27.00, Ps. An African child wakes to the wonders of her native land. Delicate watercolor and pencil drawings by Nonny Hogrogian.

Waters, Kate. *Lion Dancer: Ernie Wan's Chinese New Year*. Scholastic, 1991. 15" × 19", $24.95, Gr 1–2. Six-year-old Ernie prepares for his first Lion Dance during Chinese New Year.

Weiss, Nicki. *Surprise Box*. Scholastic, 1995. 15" × 18", $24.95, Ps–K. A cute story about a girl, a box, a ribbon, and a drawer.

———. *Where Does the Brown Bear Go?* Puffin, 1990. 15" × 18", $27.99, Ps. When the lights go down in the city, the animals find their way home.

Wells, Rosemary. *Hazel's Amazing Mother*. Dial, 1985. 14½" × 18", $17.99, Ps. When Hazel and her beloved doll Eleanor are set upon by bullies, Hazel's mother comes to the rescue in a surprising way.

———. *Noisy Nora*. Scholastic, 1993. 11¾" × 18", $28.99, Ps. Feeling neglected by her parents, Nora makes more and more noise trying to attract their attention until she gets more attention than she wants.

———. *Morris's Disappearing Bag*. Dial Books for Young Readers, 1975. 13¾" × 18", $16.95, Ps. Morris, the youngest child, is ignored by his family on Christmas morning. He is not having much fun until he discovers a gift he missed—a bag that will make him invisible.

———. *Shy Charles*. Puffin Pied Piper Giant, 1992. 13¾" × 18", $17.99, Ps. Being painfully timid and shy does not stop a young mouse from rescuing his babysitter in an emergency. But even after becoming a hero, Charles still doesn't utter a word.

Wescott, Nadine Bernard. *Peanut Butter and Jelly*. Dutton/A Puffin Unicorn, 1987. 14½" × 15½", $17.95, Ps. Rhyming text and funny illustrations explain how to make and eat a peanut butter and jelly sandwich. Hand and feet motions for the rhyme are included at the end of the book.

Whitehead, Patricia. *Best Halloween Book*. Troll, 1985. 15" × 19", $14.95, Gr 1. Annie is frightened by many things on Halloween, but on this Halloween she frightens everyone else.

———. *Best Valentine Book*. Troll, 1985. 15" × 19", $14.95, Gr 1. While Big Benny feels blue about not receiving any Valentine cards in the mail, the reader is introduced to the letters of the alphabet.

———. *Christmas Alphabet Book: An ABC Adventure*. Troll, 1985. 15" × 19", $14.95, Gr 1. While Santa belatedly leaves on his Christmas eve trip, the reader is introduced to the letters of the alphabet.

———. *Here Comes Hungry Albert*. Troll, 1985. 15" × 19", $14.95, Gr 1. No matter how much he eats, Albert the ape can always eat more. A letter from the alphabet appears on each page with an appropriate word from the text.

Williams, Rebel. *A Beaver Tale*. Wright Group, 1990. 15" × 18", $25.00, Gr 1–2. A nonfiction account of beavers building a dam, set to the tune of "The Wheels on the Bus."

Williams, Rozanne. *Buttons, Buttons*. Creative Teaching Press, 1994. 12" × 18", $7.95, Gr 1. The physical properties of buttons are explained. Eight pages. Not a primary purchase.

———. *Four Seasons*. Creative Teaching Press, 1994. 12" × 18", $7.95, Gr 1. The basic concept of the four seasons are shown with simple sentences. Eight pages. Not a primary purchase.

———. *I See Colors*. Creative Teaching Press, 1994. 12" × 18", $7.95, Gr 1. Colors are illustrated with photographs and the sentence "I see. . . ." Eight pages. Not a primary purchase.

———. *It's Melting*. Creative Teaching Press, 1994. 12" × 18", $7.95, Gr 1. A property of certain matters is melting. Shown very basically here. Eight pages. Not a primary purchase.

———. *On the Go*. Creative Teaching Press, 1994. 12" × 18", $7.95, Gr 1. Bus, car, bike, train, plane, and feet are shown as methods of transportation. Eight pages. Not a primary purchase.

———. *Reduce, Reuse, Recycle*. Creative Teaching Press, 1994. 12" × 18", $7.95, Gr 1. Multicultural kids tell the simple message of recycling to save the planet. Eight pages. Not a primary purchase.

———. *Round and Round the Seasons Go*. Creative Teaching Press, 1994. 12" × 18", $7.95, Gr 1. Circles show cartoon illustrations of the seasons. A simple but very descriptive rhyme complete this short book. Eight pages. Not a primary purchase.

———. *We Can Eat the Plants*. Creative Teaching Press, 1994. 12" × 18", $7.95, Gr 1. We can eat the roots, stems, leaves, fruit, and seeds of plants. Eight pages. Not a primary purchase.

———. *What's the Weather Like Today?* Creative Teaching Press, 1994. 12" × 18", $7.95, Gr 2. Rain, snow, sun, wind, and clouds are introduced. Eight pages. Not a primary purchase.

———. *Who Lives Here?* Creative Teaching Press, 1994. 12" × 18", $7.95, Gr 2. Habitat ecology is explained through different animals. Eight pages. Not a primary purchase.

————. *Whose Forest Is It?* Creative Teaching Press, 1994. 12" × 18", $7.95, Gr 1. Forest conservation as an important activity is explained. Eight pages. Not a primary purchase.

Williams, Sue. *I Went Walking*. HBJ/Gulliver Books, 1989. 18" × 18", $18.95, Ps. During the course of a walk, a young boy identifies animals of many different colors.

Williams, Vera B. *A Chair for My Mother*. Mulberry, 1982. 14" × 20", $18.95, Gr 1–3. A child, her waitress mother, and her grandmother save dimes to buy a comfortable chair after all their furniture is lost in a fire.

Winthrop, Elizabeth. *Shoes*. HarperCollins, 1992. 15" × 18", $19.95, Ps. A survey of all the many kinds of shoes in the world concludes that the best shoes of all are bare feet.

Wood, Audrey. *King Bidgood's in the Bathtub*. HBJ, 1993. 15" × 18", $19.95, Ps. Despite the pleas of his court, this fun-loving king refuses to get out of the bathtub and rule his kingdom.

————. *The Napping House*. HBJ, 1984. 16" × 18", $18.95, Ps. In this cumulative tale, a wakeful flea on top of a number of sleeping creatures causes a commotion with just one bite.

————. *Silly Sally*. HBJ, 1992. 15½" × 18", $19.95, Ps. Rhyming story of Sally, who makes many friends as she travels across town, backwards, and upside down.

Wood, Don, and Audrey Wood. *The Little Mouse, the Ripe, Red Strawberry, and the Big Hungry Bear*. Child's Play, 1990. 20" × 20", $24.95, Ps–2. How do you keep a bear from taking your ripe, red strawberry?

Wylie, Joanne. *A Fishy Color Story*. Children's Press, 1983. 15½" × 20", $19.99, Gr 2. A child introduces the colors while answering questions about beautiful fish. Illustrated with cut and torn paper collage.

Yamate, Sandra. *The Boy Who Loved Dumplings*. Newbridge, 1992. 14¼" × 19½", $14.99, Gr 1. Jimmy's friends do not understand his great love for eating dumpling in this multicultural tale until they taste them.

Young, Ed. *Seven Blind Mice*. Scholastic, 1994. 17" × 18¾", $19.95, Ps. A retelling of the Indian fable of seven blind men who find an elephant and argue over what it is. The arguers in this version are mice.

Ziefert, Harriet. *A Clean House for Mole and Mouse*. Scholastic, 1994. 15" × 18", $24.95, Gr K–1. From top to bottom, Mole and Mouse clean house.

Zimmerman, H. Werner. *Henny Penny*. Scholastic, 1989. 14⅞" × 17⅞", $19.95, Ps. Henny Penny and her friends are on their way to tell the king that the sky is falling when they meet a hungry fox. Illustrations by Zimmerman are quite humorous.

Big Book Publishing Sources

Addison Wesley
2725 Sand Hill Rd.
Menlo Park, CA 94025
(800) 548-4885

Aladdin (an imprint of S&S)

Beckley Cardy
1 E. First St.
Duluth, MN 55802
(800) 446-1477
fax (800) 237-4089

Bradbury (an imprint of S&S)

Celebration Press
P.O. Box 1317
Pleasant Valley, NY 12569
(914) 635-2575

Children's Press
5440 N. Cumberland Ave.
Chicago, IL 60656
(800) 621-1115

Collier (an imprint of S&S)

Crowell (an imprint of S&S)

Dial Books for Young Readers
375 Hudson St.
New York, NY 10014
(800) 526-0275

Dominie Press
5945 Pacific Center Blvd., Suite 505
San Diego, CA 92121
(800) 232-4570
fax (619) 546-8822

Dutton/Puffin/Unicorn
375 Hudson
New York, NY 10014
(212) 366-2000

Firefly
P.O. Box 1338
Ellicott Station
Buffalo, NY 14205
(800) 387-5085

Greenwillow
1350 Avenue of the Americas
New York, NY 10019
(800) 843-9389

Gulliver (an imprint of Harcourt Brace
    Jovanovich)

Harcourt Brace Jovanovich (HBJ)
525 B St., Suite 1900
San Diego, CA 92101
(800) 346-8648

HarperCollins Children's Books
10 E. 53rd St.
New York, NY 10022
(800) 331-3761

Harper Trophy (an imprint of HarperCollins)

Hawthorne Press
P.O. Box 135
Wheeling, IL 60050
(800) 823-2434

Henry Holt
115 W. 18th St.
New York, NY 10011
(800) 488-5233

Houghton Mifflin
222 Berkley St.
Boston, MA 02116
(800) 225-3363

Knopf Books for Young Readers
201 50th St.
New York, NY 10022
(800) 726-0600

Lakeshore
2695 E. Dominguez St.
P.O. Box 6261
Carson, CA 90749
(800) 421-5354
fax (310) 537-5403

Lothrop (an imprint of Morrow/Mulberry)

Macmillan Publishing Company
866 Third Ave., 25th Floor
New York, NY 10022
(800) 223-2336
fax (800) 445-6991

Milliken Publishing
1100 Research Blvd.
St. Louis, MO 63132-0579
(800) 325-4136
fax (800) 538-1319

Modern Curriculum Press
13900 Prospect Rd.
Cleveland, OH 44136
(800) 321-3106
fax (216) 572-2825

Morrow/Mulberry
1350 Avenue of the Americas
New York, NY 10019
(800) 843-9389

Nellie Edge
Box 12399
Salem, OR 97309-0399
(800) 523-4594

Newbridge
333 E. 38th St.
New York, NY 10016
(800) 867-0307

North South Books
1123 Broadway, Suite 800
New York, NY 10010
(800) 722-6657

Permabound
Vandalia Rd.
Jacksonville, IL 62650
(800) 637-6581
fax (800) 551-1169

Puffin/Pied Piper (an imprint of Dial)

Putnam
200 Madison Ave.
New York, NY 10016
(800) 631-8571

Rigby Education
P.O. Box 797
Crystal Lake, IL 60014
(800) 822-8661

Scholastic, Inc.
555 Broadway
New York, NY 10022
(800) 325-6149
fax (212) 343-4535

Simon & Schuster (S&S)
200 Old Tappan Rd.
Old Tappan, NJ 07675
(800) 223-2348

Teaching Resource Center
P.O. Box 1509
San Leandro, CA 94577
(800) 833-3389
fax (800) 972-7722

Thomas Nelson, Inc.
P.O. Box 141000
Nashville, TN 37214
(800) 251-4000

Troll
100 Corporate Dr.
Mahwah, NJ 07430
(800) 526-5289
fax (201) 529-9347

The Wright Group
19201 120th Ave.
Bothell, WA 98011-9512
(800) 523-2371
fax (206) 486-7704

Index

ads, 13
Aliki, 32

Baer, Gene, 34
bag, 13
Baker, Keith, 35
banner, 13
Barbour, Ken, 31
Barton, Byron, 25–26; 31–32
Beaver Tale, 25
Bemelmans, Ludwig, 32
Big Books:
   circulating, 10
   construction, 5
   displaying, 7–9
   equipment, 7–9
     (sources of, 11)
   format, 5
   general information, 13–24
   Kapco adhesives, 10–11
   laminating, 10
   preserving, 10–11
   publishing sources, 95–97
   quality, 5
   readings about, 73–74
   Repair Kit, 11
   selected bibliography, 75–94
   storage, 5, 7–9
   using, 13–71
book cover, 13
Brett, Jan, 32

Can't You Sleep, Little Bear?, 25
Carle, Eric, 35
Carlstrom, Nancy White, 29
Child, Lydia Marie, 33

Corduroy, 25
cube, 13, 19
Curious George, 25

Dabcovich, Lydia, 25
De Paola, Tomie, 34
Dinosaurs, Dinosaurs, 25–26
Discovery, 3–4
Doorbell Rang, The, 26
Dunbar, Joyce, 34

Each Orange Had Eight Slices, 26
Ehlert, Lois, 26–27, 33–34
Exploration, 4
Extension, 4

Feathers for Lunch, 26–27
flannel story, 13
Fleming, Denise, 29–30
Frazier, Debra, 32
Freeman, Don, 25
Freight Train, 27–28

Gelman, Rita Golden, 35
Gibbons, Gail, 32
Giganti, Paul, 26
Grossman, Bill, 35

Hazen, Barbara, 35
Hoberman, Mary Ann, 29
House is a House for Me, A, 29
How Much is a Million?, 29
Hutchins, Pat, 26

I Like Me!, 29
I Love Cats, 29

Index

In the Tall, Tall Grass, 29–30
independent experience, 5
It Looked Like Spilt Milk, 30
Itsy Bitsy Spider, The, 30–31

Jump, Frog, Jump!, 31

Kalan, Robert, 31
Keats, Ezra Jack, 34
Kellogg, Steven, 33

Little Nino's Pizzeria, 31
Little Old Woman and the Hungry Cat, The, 31
Little Red Hen, 31–32

Madeline, 32
Matthias, Catherine, 29
Milk Makers, The, 32
Mitten, The, 32
mobile, 13
Mouse Paint, 32
mural, 13
My Five Senses, 32

On the Day You Were Born, 32
Over the River and Through the Wood, 33

pantomime, 13
patterns, 15–24; 37–71
Paul Bunyan, 33
Peanut Butter and Jelly, 33
Pfister, Marcus, 34

Planting a Rainbow, 33–34
Polette, Nancy, 31
posters, 13

Rainbow Fish, The, 34
Rey, H. A., 25

Schwartz, David, 29
scientific elements, 13
selection criteria, 1–2
Shaw, Charles G., 30
Snowy Day, 34
stick puppets, 13
Stoll, Ellen W., 32
Strega Nona, 34

Ten Little Mice, 34
Thump, Thump, Rat-a-Tat-Tat, 34
Tommy at the Grocery Store, 35
Trapani, Iza, 30–31
travel poster, 13

Very Hungry Caterpillar, The, 35

Waddell, Martin, 25
Weiss, Nicki, 35
Wescott, Nadine, 33
Where Does the Brown Bear Go?, 35
Who Is the Beast?, 35
Who Lost a Shoe?, 35
Why Can't I Fly?, 35

About the Author

Robin Works Davis is the youth services supervisor at the Farmers Branch Manske Library in Farmers Branch, Texas, and an adjunct professor in children's literature at the University of North Texas. She obtained her Bachelor of Fine Arts degree from Baylor University and her Masters in Information Science from the University of North Texas. She is a member of the Texas Library Association, ALA, International Reading Association, and Kappa Delta Sorority Alumni Association. In 1993 and 1997 she received the ALSC/Book Wholesalers National Reading Program Grant. She also received a special award in 1997 for her Reading Club Program from the Captain Planet Foundation, a grant from the Ronald McDonald Foundation for library outreach to babies, and has received the Ezra Jack Keats minigrant twice. Davis has also done extensive consulting on programming and literature.

She is the author of three Reading Club Manuals for the State of Texas, as well as *Invent the Future: Read!; The Incredible Dream Machine* (Texas State Library, 1997) and *Camp Wanna-Read* (Texas State Library, 1991). She is also the author of *Promoting Reading through Reading Programs* (Neal Schuman, 1992), *An Alphabet of Books* (Highsmith Press, 1994), *An Alphabet of Authors* (Highsmith Press, 1996), *Art and Children: Using Literature to Expand Creativity* (Scarecrow Press, 1996), *Toddle on Over* (Highsmith Press, 1998) and *Multimedia Storytimes* (Highsmith Press, forthcoming).